ETHICAL INFIDELITY

Why Cheating Is More Faithful Than
You Think

JULIAN VALE

"One must be faithful to the dream, not to the person."

— *Jeanne Moreau (via Louis Malle's La Notte*)**

"Faithfulness is not an act of memory, but of imagination."

— *Friedrich Nietzsche (The Gay Science, paraphrased)*

"The task of ethics is not to make us pure, but to make us responsible."

— *Emmanuel Levinas*

Table of Contents

Introduction:
The Scandal of the Question

The Scandal of the Question

A man sits alone in a hotel room. He isn't young, and he isn't reckless. The carpet smells faintly of cleaning chemicals, the air-conditioner hums with the nervous steadiness of a machine trying too hard. On the table beside him lie his car keys, his phone turned facedown, and his wedding ring, which he turns slowly between his fingers as though it were an artifact he must interpret. His marriage is not unhappy. At home is a woman he still loves in the most durable sense of the word — love as daily commitment, as shared memory, as something closer to kinship than to heat. They have lived through illness, financial strain, childbirth, and the small humiliations that accompany familiarity. They have forgiven each other for the usual human things: carelessness, anger, the dull cruelty of routine. By all appearances, he is a good man, and this is a good marriage.

And yet, tonight, he will cross a line. He has told himself a story to justify it — that it will mean nothing, that no one will be hurt, that it is only a small correction to the vast asymmetry between who he is and who he was once allowed to be. He does not expect transcendence. He wants relief: from repetition, from the stifling predictability of being known too well, from the quiet fear that life's richest sensations have already been spent. He does not despise his wife. He fears, rather, that the slow erosion of desire will make him despise himself.

He knows, of course, that what he is about to do will be called betrayal. Our culture offers no ambiguity here. We are told that infidelity is the definitive moral crime of intimacy: the shattering of trust, the rupture from which love cannot recover. Entire genres — novels, films, self-help manuals — exist to reinforce this consensus. To cheat is to fail at love; to forgive it is to lack dignity. Yet beneath this moral absolutism lies an uncomfortable truth: people continue to cheat, and not all of them are villains. Many are people like the man in the hotel room — loyal in every other sense, carrying the contradiction between affection and appetite like a private wound.

The question this book asks is not whether betrayal hurts — it does — but whether the moral story we tell about it captures the full complexity of human love. We pretend that fidelity and goodness are identical, that to remain faithful is to be virtuous and to stray is to be corrupt. But life resists such arithmetic. Fidelity can conceal cowardice; infidelity can conceal tenderness. Some affairs destroy families, but others preserve them by allowing desire to survive in exile, protecting a marriage from the slow suffocation of unfulfilled need. Perhaps, sometimes, secrecy is less a lie than a form of mercy.

The man in the hotel room is not exceptional. He is simply living out a tension that defines modern intimacy: the desire for both security and freedom, the need to feel anchored and the equal need to feel alive. The vows of monogamy promise peace, but they also demand renunciation — of curiosity, of risk, of the thrill of possibility. To remain entirely faithful is to choose stability over discovery; to stray is to risk chaos for the sake of renewal. The tragedy is that both choices carry their own kind of loss.

To even ask whether this act might be *ethical* feels indecent, as though the question itself were a betrayal. But ethics, if it means anything at all, is the art of thinking clearly about difficult things. And what could be more human, or more difficult, than the attempt to reconcile love's two demands: the need to belong to someone, and the need to remain free?

This is the scandal of the question that follows through this book:

Can there be such a thing as *ethical infidelity* — an act that violates a rule but remains faithful to love's deeper truth?

The Moral Orthodoxy

Few subjects provoke such unanimous certainty as infidelity. In a moral landscape increasingly fractured — where truth is negotiable, institutions are distrusted, and even virtue itself feels provisional — the condemnation of cheating remains one of the last points of common faith. It unites the conservative and the liberal, the religious and the secular. To cheat is to break the primordial law of intimacy: *thou shalt not betray the one who loves you.*

Our collective imagination treats this law as self-evident. We grow up inside stories that confirm it — novels that punish adulterers with madness or death, films that end with exposure and humiliation, songs that equate fidelity with goodness and straying with shame. Even our language makes moral judgment inescapable: we "cheat," we "sneak," we "stray." Each word carries its own miniature sermon. The unfaithful partner is a liar by definition, an actor wearing the mask of devotion while rehearsing betrayal.

Yet this moral orthodoxy has a curious rigidity. It leaves no space for gradation, no recognition that desire and affection can coexist in tension rather than opposition. It insists on a binary: faithful or unfaithful, saint or sinner. We moralize intimacy the way earlier ages moralized hunger — as something to be controlled, purified, tamed. But where appetite for food is granted its rhythms and excesses, sexual and emotional appetite are cast as moral tests of character. To admit ambivalence is to risk condemnation.

Part of the force of this orthodoxy lies in its simplicity. It offers the reassurance that love, if pure, will immunize us against temptation. Fidelity becomes proof of moral integrity; infidelity, proof of decay. We want this to be true because it makes the fragile machinery of intimacy seem governable. But the promise is a false one. Even the happiest marriages know the flicker of curiosity, the fleeting fantasy, the yearning for a self unbound by history. To acknowledge this is not to cheapen love, but to see it honestly.

And yet, we live in denial. We preserve the ideal by shrouding its failures in secrecy and shame. When infidelity is discovered, we treat it as revelation — the sudden unveiling of corruption — rather than as one possible expression of the contradictions built into monogamy itself. The moral outrage that follows often serves less to protect love than to protect our faith in the ideal that love should be simple, self-sufficient, and eternally new.

What this orthodoxy cannot bear is ambiguity: the possibility that an act might wound and yet sustain, that concealment might coexist with care. It has no grammar for the lover who cheats not out of contempt but out of fear — fear of dullness, of invisibility, of desire's extinction. To admit such complexity would require us to see infidelity not as a moral aberration but as a human response to the difficulty of remaining alive within commitment.

This book begins from that discomfort. It does not ask the reader to abandon the moral intuitions that make fidelity meaningful. It asks only that we hold them against the stubborn facts of human nature — that love can coexist with transgression, that secrecy can sometimes protect what truth might destroy, and that the ethics of intimacy may not always align with its rules.

The Hidden Contradiction

If the moral orthodoxy tells us that fidelity is the highest proof of love, human experience quietly tells another story. Monogamy promises peace, but it also manufactures the conditions of its own crisis. Its stability depends on a fantasy it cannot fulfill: that desire, once anchored in devotion, will remain eternally self-sufficient.

Desire does not obey vows. It feeds on novelty, distance, and risk — the very elements monogamy is designed to neutralize. What begins as erotic mystery becomes familiarity; what once thrilled becomes routine. The same partner who once appeared as an undiscovered continent becomes a well-mapped landscape. Love may deepen, but erotic curiosity rarely vanishes; it simply seeks other outlets. The result is a quiet contradiction built into the institution itself: we are asked to sustain passion in conditions that extinguish it.

Modern culture amplifies this tension. We are told to make our partners our best friends, co-parents, therapists, and lovers — to combine domestic serenity with unending sexual novelty. It is a heroic ideal, but one almost no one can meet. Psychologists like Esther Perel have described how couples confuse security with desire, expecting the same relationship to offer both safety and surprise. But safety and surprise pull in opposite directions: the more we know someone, the harder it becomes to be thrilled by them; the more we depend on them, the more frightening it is to risk destabilizing that bond. Desire, which thrives on uncertainty, withers under total transparency.

This contradiction does not prove that monogamy is wrong. It shows, rather, that it is tragic — an arrangement that demands from us a discipline nature never guaranteed. We ask the body to ignore its chemistry, the imagination to ignore its wanderings, the heart to treat constancy as its only language. For some, this works; for most, it does not. What follows are small evasions: pornography, flirtations, fantasies, emotional affairs conducted through screens. We call these compromises "harmless," yet we condemn the physical act that at least acknowledges the truth those evasions only simulate — that desire does not vanish, it migrates.

The moral orthodoxy condemns the act of betrayal but excuses the thousand tiny alienations that precede it: the silent withdrawal, the emotional numbness, the nightly scrolling through pornography that replaces intimacy with simulation. But if we measure harm honestly, which is the greater betrayal — the discreet act that restores vitality, or the long erosion that leaves both partners diminished? The contradiction of monogamy is not that it forbids cheating, but that it forbids the very restlessness that makes fidelity meaningful.

The Philosophical Premise

To speak of *ethical infidelity* is to enter philosophy through its oldest doorway: the problem of moral absolutes. From the beginning, moral philosophy has wrestled with the question of whether right and wrong are fixed categories or whether they depend on circumstance, intention, and consequence. Monogamy, in its modern moral form, belongs to the world of absolutes. It divides the moral landscape with a clean blade: fidelity on one side, betrayal on the other. The commandment is categorical, not conditional.

But human life, as philosophers from Aristotle to Simone Weil have observed, rarely fits clean categories. We live among competing goods: love and freedom, stability and vitality, honesty and kindness. Every moral choice, in this light, is a negotiation between imperfect options. What matters is not the purity of the rule but the balance of its consequences.

From this perspective, *ethical infidelity* becomes thinkable. It does not mean that betrayal ceases to wound, but that the act's moral weight depends on its intention and effects. John Stuart Mill would recognize this logic: his harm principle holds that the morality of an action rests not on its conformity to rules but on whether it causes or prevents suffering. If a discreet act of infidelity protects a family, sustains tenderness, and averts bitterness, then the calculus of harm may look different from the moral slogans that condemn it outright.

Other traditions sharpen the paradox further. The ethics of care, developed by thinkers like Carol Gilligan and Virginia Held, argues that morality is not a matter of universal rules but of sustaining the fragile webs of relationship upon which human life depends. From that vantage point, an act of infidelity can be evaluated not by its violation of a code but by its impact on care. Does it preserve the relationship's ecology — its mutual support, its daily kindness — or does it corrode it?

At the opposite pole stands Nietzsche, for whom morality is often the mask of resentment — a way for the weak to shame the strong for their vitality. From his standpoint, monogamy's moral absolutism is less an ethical triumph than a triumph of repression: the taming of instinct, the denial of life's multiplicity. "You have made a virtue of your bondage," he might say, "and called it fidelity." In Nietzsche's view, the question is not whether one breaks a rule, but whether one affirms life. The ethical act is the one that preserves the capacity for creation, energy, and becoming — even if it scandalizes the herd.

Strangely, one could even enlist more conservative voices in this argument. Ayn Rand, who preached the integrity of the self above all else, might see "ethical infidelity" as a paradoxical defense of authenticity — a refusal to live a lie in the name of convention. For her, virtue lies in acting in accordance with one's values and desires, so long as one accepts responsibility for the consequences. The moral failure, in that framework, would not be the act of cheating itself, but the act of cowardice: to live divided between what one feels and what one performs.

Each of these philosophical perspectives converges on a shared insight: ethics begins where rules end. It is not the avoidance of contradiction but the ability to inhabit it consciously. The problem with moral orthodoxy is not that it upholds fidelity, but that it refuses to see the complexity of what fidelity entails. Love is not only a promise; it is a practice sustained amid competing imperatives — intimacy and individuality, truth and protection, eros and peace.

The question, then, is not whether infidelity is wrong in the abstract. It is whether, in the lived reality of human bonds, there can exist acts that violate the rule of monogamy but remain faithful to love's deeper logic: care, mercy, and the preservation of vitality. That is the philosophical premise of this book — and the paradox it will explore in all its danger, nuance, and necessity.

The Broader Cultural Frame

Every age moralizes its contradictions in its own language. Ours happens to speak the dialect of therapy, confession, and self-optimization. We inhabit a culture that treats intimacy as both a refuge and a project — something to be managed, maintained, and improved. Love has become a form of work, requiring constant emotional fluency, transparency, and accountability. The modern couple is expected to be two sovereign individuals who freely choose monogamy and then endlessly renegotiate its terms. What was once enforced from outside by religion or community is now policed from within, by conscience and confession.

It is a paradox that Esther Perel has captured with unusual clarity. In *Mating in Captivity*, she argues that the modern ideal of intimacy — total honesty, total sharing, total safety — inadvertently extinguishes the erotic imagination that first drew two people together. Desire, she reminds us, needs distance; mystery is its oxygen. Yet our culture treats secrecy as a pathology, not a condition of longing. We demand from love both the security of home and the adventure of the unknown, and when the two collapse into each other, we are left bewildered by our own boredom.

Technology has magnified the contradiction to almost unbearable proportions. The smartphone renders temptation omnipresent: every message, image, and notification is a small invitation to imagine otherwise. The same devices that connect couples also exhaust them, dissolving boundaries between private and public, work and intimacy, fantasy and fidelity. We now live in an attention economy where desire itself has become a form of currency. Pornography is infinite; dating apps transform flirtation into metrics. Monogamy, in this context, is not only a moral discipline but an act of resistance against distraction.

And yet, the more we attempt to discipline desire, the more it escapes into other forms. The hunger for risk that once animated eros reappears in other registers: overwork, gambling, compulsive consumption, doomscrolling. These are the moral descendants of the old affair — attempts to feel something vivid in a life anesthetized by safety. The modern subject, especially the modern man, is expected to be domesticated yet ambitious, emotionally intelligent yet stoic, endlessly productive yet self-aware. When he fails to reconcile these demands, he seeks release wherever it will appear: in fantasy, intoxication, or transgression.

What the culture condemns as "cheating" may therefore be only one expression of a broader malaise — the exhaustion of selves asked to be both secure and spontaneous, faithful and free. It is telling that so much of our storytelling revolves around the man torn between two lives: Tony Soprano, Don Draper, Walter White, and their many descendants. They are not simply symbols of male weakness; they are figures of existential strain, living in worlds that demand conformity but worship vitality. Their betrayals are never only sexual. They are groping for an authenticity the social order no longer seems to offer.

This is not to romanticize betrayal, but to recognize that the moral panic around infidelity often conceals a deeper anxiety about freedom itself. In a culture that prizes disclosure, the very notion of private transgression becomes intolerable. We are asked to be transparent to our partners, to our therapists, to our followers. But complete transparency is a fantasy — and perhaps an inhuman one. To love another person requires not the abolition of secrecy, but the ability to live with what cannot be fully known.

This book unfolds from that tension. It is not a manual for deception, nor a celebration of recklessness, but an inquiry into how modern intimacy has become so brittle that even the smallest act of mystery feels like betrayal. If the moral orthodoxy insists that love and secrecy cannot coexist, perhaps the challenge of our time is to rediscover how they might — not in the name of selfishness, but in defense of the complexity that makes love worth preserving.

The Promise of the Argument

This book begins from a simple but unsettling intuition: that fidelity, as we usually understand it, is too narrow a measure for love. We have mistaken obedience for devotion, transparency for honesty, constancy for care. In doing so, we have made monogamy not a practice of love but a test of character — a moral performance that often conceals more fear than virtue. The question of *ethical infidelity* is therefore not a provocation for its own sake; it is a way of asking what love itself demands when the tidy categories of good and evil fall apart.

To approach the subject this way is to accept that love is tragic. Every choice it offers comes at the expense of something else: freedom for safety, novelty for security, mystery for knowledge. The wish to reconcile these opposites — to have both peace and passion, permanence and surprise — is the emotional fantasy on which modern intimacy is built. But fantasies exact a price. When they fail, we lash out at the wrong target, moralizing the symptom rather than examining the structure that produces it.

The chapters that follow move between philosophy, history, psychology, and culture. They begin with biology and anthropology, showing that monogamy is not a law of nature but a social invention, and then turn to its ethical promise — the depth, stability, and equality it alone can offer. From there, the argument threads through the contradictions of modern life: our obsession with confession, our hunger for escape, our need for vitality in an age of safety. It draws on thinkers as different as Mill, Nietzsche, Rand, and Perel; on the cautionary fictions of *Anna Karenina* and *Mad Men*; on the everyday tragedies that unfold in bedrooms, offices, and hotel rooms across the world.

This is not a defense of deceit, nor an apology for betrayal. It is an attempt to describe the moral reality of love as it is lived rather than idealized. *Ethical infidelity* is not a slogan but a framework for thinking about how desire and care coexist within the same heart, how secrecy can sometimes serve tenderness, how a small act of transgression can preserve what duty alone might destroy.

If the orthodox morality of fidelity tells us that love thrives only in the light, this book asks what might also grow in the shadows — the quiet mercies, the necessary silences, the compromises that make longevity possible. Its wager is that fidelity is not a matter of rule-following but of discernment: knowing when to hold firm, when to bend, and when breaking the letter of a promise might keep its spirit alive.

In the end, the argument is neither cynical nor libertine. It is, paradoxically, a defense of love's seriousness — of the belief that to remain truly faithful, one must sometimes have the courage to betray.

Chapter 1:
"Are Humans Naturally Monogamous?"

Pair-Bonding and the Puzzle of Exclusivity

Humans are not solitary creatures. We are born helpless, raised in groups, and wired for attachment. The infant's cry seeks not food alone but presence; the adult's longing for love is an echo of that original dependency. Across the millennia, this impulse toward connection has produced what biologists call *pair-bonding*— the tendency of two individuals to form a lasting emotional alliance that extends beyond reproduction. But the mystery of human love lies in what came next: we transformed a biological attachment into a moral demand. From the instinct to bond we derived the commandment to remain exclusive.

In evolutionary terms, pair-bonding is pragmatic. Species that depend on extended parental care—wolves, some birds, certain primates—develop it as a strategy for survival. The bond keeps two caregivers near the nest long enough for the offspring to live. In humans, whose infants remain dependent for years, the pair-bond became unusually strong, reinforced by hormones such as oxytocin and vasopressin, the chemical signatures of trust and closeness. These substances create the soft focus through which lovers see each other: the sense that this one person, among billions, matters absolutely. Nature's trick is elegant—she disguises duty as devotion.

Yet biology offers no guarantee that the bond will remain sexually exclusive. Emotional attachment and erotic desire, though often intertwined, follow different clocks. The hormones that sustain closeness plateau over time; the ones that ignite desire thrive on novelty. We can stay attached to a partner for decades while the currents of attraction drift elsewhere. Where attachment seeks repetition, desire seeks surprise. The very stability that love builds threatens the restlessness that first brought it into being.

Philosophers have long intuited this split. Aristotle distinguished *philia*, the friendship rooted in shared life, from *eros*, the appetite that disrupts it. *Philia* is steady, ethical, and civilizing; *eros* is wild, disruptive, and creative. Civilization depends on the former but is periodically renewed by the latter. To live as a pair is to be suspended between the two, negotiating a treaty between domestic peace and erotic revolt.

Modern monogamy tries to reconcile them—to build a lifelong institution on the foundation of an emotion designed for flux. It asks *eros* to become a citizen. But desire resists domestication. However ardently we pledge exclusivity, some part of the self remains curious about the unknown, alert to difference. This is not proof of corruption; it is a sign of vitality. The capacity to be moved by another face, another voice, is part of what makes us human. Fidelity, then, is not the absence of temptation but the art of managing it.

Recognizing this distinction—between pair-bonding as attachment and exclusivity as ideal—does not cheapen love. It clarifies it. Our bonds are real, our loyalties profound, but they are sustained by effort, not instinct. The moral drama of monogamy begins where nature ends: in the work of choosing, again and again, to remain.

Male Desire and Evolutionary Incentives

If attachment binds, desire disperses. It seeks not safety but risk, not repetition but renewal. This tension is universal, but it manifests differently across sexes, and it is here—within the architecture of male desire—that one of monogamy's deepest instabilities resides.

From an evolutionary perspective, the male body was not designed for scarcity. It produces sperm by the millions, a biological hint of abundance and dispersal. The logic, brutally simple, is one of probability: the more partners a man impregnates, the greater the chance his genes survive. Over millennia this arithmetic shaped instincts—curiosity about novelty, a sharpened eye for youth and fertility, a quick ignition of lust followed by rapid satiation. In many species these impulses express themselves without restraint; in humans, they are filtered through culture, ethics, and imagination, but they do not disappear.

The behavioral biologists call it the *Coolidge effect*: the observation that males of many mammals exhibit renewed sexual interest when introduced to a novel partner, even after losing interest in a familiar one. It is not a moral failure but a neural reflex—dopamine's preference for what it has not yet conquered. The tragedy, for human beings, is that the same brain built for the thrill of discovery must also sustain the patience of devotion.

But biology explains impulse, not destiny. To recognize an evolutionary pattern is not to endorse it. The capacity for self-control, for ethical choice, is what distinguishes instinct from conduct. What is troubling is not that men feel temptation but that modern culture has flattened their imaginative possibilities for release. In earlier epochs, risk and adventure were scattered through the landscape of work and survival—through hunting, warfare, exploration. Desire for the new could be sublimated into danger or creation. In a world domesticated by safety and routine, that surplus energy often finds narrower exits: pornography, gambling, addiction, compulsive achievement.

This is why moral absolutism around fidelity often fails men without educating them. It tells them what not to do without giving them a language for what they feel. To be told that temptation is evil is to learn to lie about it. To be told that fidelity is proof of goodness is to make desire synonymous with guilt. The result is repression, followed by hypocrisy, followed by collapse. When men eventually transgress, they do so not with mindfulness but with despair, confusing secrecy with freedom and punishment with renewal.

The discipline of monogamy, then, should not be understood as the suppression of instinct but as its redirection. It demands an art of management rather than denial: the channeling of the restless energies that once served survival into forms that can sustain intimacy rather than destroy it. Some find that art through fantasy, others through sublimation, a few through carefully bounded transgression. Whatever form it takes, the ethical task remains the same—to acknowledge that the drive for novelty is real, and that its denial without understanding breeds only deceit.

To love faithfully in such conditions is not to be untempted but to engage temptation consciously, even compassionately. It is to see male desire not as sin but as a force to be domesticated without being extinguished, to turn the ancient restlessness of the hunter into a more delicate kind of pursuit: the search for vitality within commitment.

The Human Spectrum: Lessons from Other Primates

When biologists search for clues about human nature, they often turn to our closest relatives. The primate family is a living archive of evolutionary experiments in sex and society. Some species pair for life; others mate in brief, frenzied exchanges. Some males guard mates jealously; others compete by producing more potent sperm. There is no single "natural" model—only strategies tuned to different environments. To understand why human fidelity is so fraught, it helps to see where we sit on this spectrum.

Our cousins, the chimpanzees, live in large, mixed groups where females mate with many males. Paternity is uncertain, but alliances are strong, and dominance depends on charisma as much as brute force. Their social chaos produces a strange peace: when everyone mates with everyone, jealousy has little ground to grow. At the other extreme are the gibbons, small tree-dwellers who form long-term pairs. They sing duets, share territory, and raise offspring together—but even they are not paragons of virtue. DNA studies show that a portion of gibbon young are fathered by outsiders. Fidelity, it seems, is an aspiration, not a guarantee.

Then there are the bonobos, whose societies are governed less by aggression than by pleasure. For them, sex is communication—a way to resolve conflict, forge bonds, and diffuse tension. They use intimacy as diplomacy, turning what humans moralize into a social lubricant. The bonobo's genius is not chastity but fluidity.

Humans share features with all three. Like gibbons, we form enduring pair-bonds and invest heavily in raising young. Like chimpanzees, we experience competition and status anxiety; like bonobos, we use sexuality to create connection and ease tension. We are, in effect, a mixed-strategy species. We fall in love, pair up, and dream of permanence—but we also flirt, fantasize, and stray. Our biology is ambivalent because our environment has always been unpredictable: long childhoods demand cooperation, while mortality and mobility reward flexibility.

Anthropologists studying hunter-gatherer societies find the same variety. Among the Hadza of Tanzania or the !Kung of southern Africa, monogamy is common but serial—partnerships endure for years, then dissolve without stigma. In agricultural and pastoral societies, where property and lineage became central, sexual control tightened. Monogamy was less about morality than about inheritance: fidelity ensured that a man's heirs were truly his own. In matrilineal cultures, where descent followed the mother's line, sexual freedom expanded again. The moral codes surrounding desire were never universal; they were economic, political, and ecological adaptations.

What this mosaic of evidence reveals is that "naturalness" is a poor moral guide. Nature offers us options, not orders. The capacity to bond deeply and the capacity to wander are both ours by inheritance. Each culture chooses how to balance them, and each individual must negotiate that balance anew. The jealousy that torments the faithful and the curiosity that tempts the unfaithful are not opposing forces but twin expressions of our social intelligence—the desire to belong and the desire to be free.

When we call monogamy "unnatural," we are half right. What is unnatural is not love itself but the expectation that one person can permanently satisfy every register of our emotional and erotic life. To expect that is to forget what evolution actually gave us: not a fixed script, but a repertoire. Civilization asks us to play only one melody from that score, yet the rest of the notes hum underneath, waiting to be heard.

Why Fidelity Must Be Enforced — and Why That Matters

If biology supplies our impulses, it is culture that builds the fences. The story of fidelity begins not in nature but in the human attempt to master it. For most of our history, monogamy was less a moral ideal than a social invention—an arrangement designed to regulate power, inheritance, and cooperation. Its endurance owes less to purity than to pragmatism.

Early human communities depended on stability. To raise children who required years of care, to share scarce resources, to temper rivalry, they needed ways to channel the volatile energies of desire into predictable forms. Pair-bonding offered an answer: a contract, explicit or tacit, that linked sex, labor, and kinship. By binding erotic attachment to economic and parental partnership, societies could convert the chaos of mating into the order of family. What began as strategy hardened into norm; what was once enforced by circumstance became enforced by law.

The ancient world codified this order through religion and ritual. Marriage ceremonies sanctified possession and alliance; fidelity became the proof of legitimacy. The patriarchal logic was crude but effective: if women's sexuality could be contained, lineage could be traced, property secured, and male cooperation sustained. Civilization's first great moral breakthrough, then, was also an act of containment. It turned desire—a wild, renewable resource—into a scarce commodity managed by custom.

With time, monogamy acquired new meanings. Christianity moralized it; Romanticism idealized it; capitalism privatized it. What had begun as a social technology became a story about love itself: the belief that exclusivity is the highest expression of devotion. We no longer police fidelity for the sake of inheritance; we police it for the sake of identity. To be faithful is to prove one's worthiness, to be unfaithful is to become a moral exile. Yet the emotional absolutism of modern love hides the historical truth that fidelity was never natural—it had to be learned, practiced, imposed.

This is not to say that monogamy is a fraud. Its very artificiality is part of its dignity. What makes fidelity meaningful is that it resists instinct. It represents humanity's wager that discipline can refine desire rather than extinguish it. To commit to one person in a world of options is to turn a biological tendency into an ethical choice. It is a small act of civilization, a rebellion against the randomness of appetite. The moral beauty of monogamy lies precisely in its difficulty.

And yet, that difficulty never disappears. The drives it suppresses continue to pulse beneath the surface, producing the inevitable ruptures that keep moralists employed and novelists inspired. When those ruptures occur, we condemn them as failures of will, but they are also reminders of what monogamy costs. Every culture that celebrates fidelity must build systems—legal, religious, emotional—to maintain it, because left to our own devices, we oscillate between attachment and adventure. The need for enforcement reveals both the fragility and the grandeur of the project.

To say that fidelity must be enforced is not to argue against it. It is to see it clearly: as a cultural achievement, not a law of nature; as a discipline of love, not its spontaneous overflow. Monogamy civilizes us by asking the impossible—and in the gap between our instincts and our ideals, the entire drama of intimacy unfolds.

In the chapters that follow, we will trace how that drama took its modern form: how monogamy evolved from pragmatic alliance into moral creed, how it became both a refuge and a cage, and why the desire to break its rules may sometimes arise not from contempt for love but from the longing to keep it alive.

Chapter 2:
The Invention of Monogamy

From Property to Promise

Every institution begins as a solution to a problem. Before it became the language of love, marriage was a technology for survival — a contract forged in hunger, alliance, and fear. The earliest human settlements, emerging from the instability of nomadic life, required new forms of order: ways to distribute labor, secure inheritance, and regulate reproduction. Monogamy, in this context, was less a moral achievement than an administrative one. It solved a logistical question: how to ensure that a man's offspring were truly his, and that his property — land, livestock, lineage — would pass unchallenged to them.

The first marriage contracts were therefore acts of governance. In Mesopotamia's Code of Hammurabi, fidelity was a clause in an economic charter; the wife's chastity protected the purity of trade and bloodline. Among the ancient Hebrews, laws in *Deuteronomy* and *Leviticus* framed adultery not as a betrayal of affection but as a theft of patriarchal property. The female body was the vessel of legitimacy; her fidelity, the ledger of inheritance. The moral vocabulary of sin had not yet arrived — only the pragmatic arithmetic of ownership and control.

Yet even in these early arrangements, the emotional residue of attachment lingered. To live as a pair, however contractual, was to risk affection. What began as alliance sometimes ripened into companionship, and with companionship came the faint shadow of mutuality. In this sense, monogamy's moral potential was hidden within its utilitarian birth: an institution designed to contain desire slowly became one capable of deepening it. The miracle — or irony — of civilization is that we built the cage before we imagined the bird that might sing inside it.

As societies grew more complex, the politics of reproduction required subtler management. The emergence of agriculture and private property bound men to land and lineage; women's bodies became the conduits of both. Inheritance demanded certainty, and certainty demanded surveillance. Thus fidelity, enforced by custom, violence, and shame, became a pillar of early order. The institution worked — perhaps too well. The emotional and sexual asymmetry it produced would endure for centuries: men with concubines and courtesans, women bound by virtue and punishment. The double standard was not a flaw in the design; it was the design.

And yet, over time, another story began to stir beneath the surface — a slow moral rebellion from within the institution itself. Once the basic needs of survival were secured, people began to ask whether fidelity could mean something more than possession. The *promise* began to replace the *property*: the idea that two people might remain together not because custom required it, but because affection or duty made it meaningful. The vows that once guaranteed obedience began, tentatively, to express devotion. In that shift — from external enforcement to internal commitment — the moral idea of fidelity was born.

This transition marks one of civilization's quiet revolutions. The first empires regulated marriage to stabilize power; later ages would inherit the structure but forget its rationale. We came to believe that monogamy was sacred because it was moral, not because it was useful. The property contract transformed into covenant, the wife into partner, the household into the stage of personal virtue. A structure built to control inheritance evolved into one that defined identity itself.

It is worth pausing to note what was gained and what was lost. Fidelity as possession protected social order but denied freedom. Fidelity as promise invited equality but imposed idealism. When ownership gave way to love, the stakes of betrayal changed: infidelity ceased to be a crime against property and became a wound to the soul. What once violated the law now violated meaning. To cheat no longer endangered lineage but identity.

This is the paradox we inherit. The moral grandeur of modern monogamy — its insistence that love be voluntary, personal, and complete — is built upon foundations of control and exclusion. The institution's evolution from property to promise was not a clean replacement but an accumulation. Beneath every declaration of eternal love still lies the ancient calculus of belonging. The ring that signifies equality once marked possession; the vow that consecrates freedom still echoes the language of ownership.

To understand monogamy as invention, not revelation, is to recognize both its fragility and its brilliance. It is a cultural scaffold we continue to inhabit, even as its original architecture shows through the paint. We may no longer marry to secure land or lineage, but we still marry to secure meaning. The difference is that now we must supply the belief ourselves.

What began as a property claim became a moral promise — a metamorphosis that elevated fidelity from necessity to virtue, and in doing so, bound it to the deepest longings of the human heart. The next transformation, in the age of Christianity, would go further still: it would make monogamy not merely the moral order of society but the spiritual order of the soul.

The Moralization of Marriage

By the time Christianity began its slow conquest of the Roman world, marriage was already a versatile institution. In pagan antiquity it had served civic and social ends: a way to produce heirs, secure alliances, and manage domestic economies. The Greeks saw it as a duty to the polis; the Romans, as an instrument of empire. Fidelity was honored, but only as one virtue among others, and rarely symmetrical. Husbands might consort freely with slaves or courtesans; wives were to be chaste for reasons of lineage and decorum. Infidelity was not sin but scandal — an offense against status, not against God.

Christianity upended this order by moralizing the private life. Where the ancients had treated sexual discipline as a matter of honor or hygiene, the Church treated it as a matter of salvation. The passions were no longer appetites to be moderated; they were temptations to be purified. What began as social pragmatism became metaphysical drama.

The apostle **Paul**, writing to the Corinthians, framed marriage as a concession to weakness: "It is better to marry than to burn." In that line lies the dual inheritance of Christian monogamy — marriage as both refuge and restraint. Desire was acknowledged but mistrusted, its only legitimate outlet the narrow corridor of wedlock. To be faithful was not simply to be loyal to a partner but to participate in a divine order that demanded constancy as proof of grace.

Later theologians deepened the moral logic. Saint Augustine, haunted by his own youthful sensuality, made chastity the cornerstone of spiritual discipline. For him, the body's pleasures were reminders of humanity's fallen state. Fidelity, therefore, was not merely a social good but a penitential act — a way of turning the disorder of flesh into an image of the soul's submission to God. The faithful spouse mirrored the faithful believer; the adulterer, like the heretic, pursued false idols. The bed became an altar; sex, when sanctioned, a sacrament; love, when restrained, a path to redemption.

This moralization did something profound to the meaning of intimacy. It internalized enforcement. The earlier systems had relied on law, custom, and surveillance; now the boundary moved inside the self. Sin could occur in thought as much as in deed. The gaze became guilty, the fantasy suspect. A man no longer needed witnesses to feel condemned; he carried the tribunal within. Monogamy thus became the first modern morality — an interior discipline that anticipated the psychological conscience of later centuries.

But this spiritual elevation came at a price. By making fidelity synonymous with virtue, the Church also made desire synonymous with guilt. To feel tempted was to fail. The body's ordinary rhythms — curiosity, longing, arousal — were recast as symptoms of moral disorder. Love was sanctified only when domesticated; pleasure was tolerated only when obedient. In binding the erotic to the ethical, Christianity dignified marriage but impoverished sexuality.

Still, this fusion of piety and affection had unexpected effects. It gave marriage a new dignity — no longer a mere household contract but a moral vocation. The mutual fidelity of husband and wife became an earthly reflection of divine fidelity. To be loyal was to imitate God's constancy; to be adulterous was to mirror humankind's rebellion. In this way, the Church rescued companionship from the cold arithmetic of property, even as it chained it to the burden of sin.

By the late Middle Ages, the doctrine had softened into ritual. Weddings moved from family arrangements to ecclesiastical ceremonies; the priest replaced the patriarch. The vows that once bound households now bound souls. The word *sacramentum* — oath — fused law and love into one indissoluble bond. Monogamy had ceased to be a matter of custom; it had become a matter of faith.

31

From this point onward, the history of marriage is the history of guilt and grace entwined. The promise that once secured inheritance now secured salvation; the breach that once threatened lineage now threatened identity. Fidelity became the measure of moral worth, and infidelity the archetype of sin. We still live with this inheritance. Every modern betrayal, even in the most secular hearts, carries the echo of the confessional — the fear not only of hurting another but of falling from grace.

The next transformation would occur not in the church but in the imagination. Having moralized fidelity, the West would soon romanticize it. What theology once demanded from obedience, the modern heart would begin to demand from feeling. Love itself would become the new religion, with monogamy as its creed and passion as its prayer.

Romantic Love and the Cult of the One

When the moral world of Christendom began to loosen, the faith it had inspired did not vanish—it migrated. The sacred moved from heaven to the heart. What religion once demanded through obedience, modern love began to demand through feeling. The vow survived, but its authority changed source: fidelity no longer testified to God's constancy, but to passion's depth. To love one person totally, to be consumed by that love, became the new proof of moral seriousness. In this transposition lay the birth of modern monogamy as an inner creed—the private religion of the soul.

The roots of this transformation stretch back to the late Middle Ages, when the troubadours of Provence began to sing of an impossible love. Their poetry invented *amour courtois*, "courtly love," a devotion not to one's spouse but to an unattainable lady. This love was erotic, illicit, and ennobling—a rebellion against arranged marriage and the utilitarian order of the household. It introduced an idea that would define the next five centuries: that love, to be worthy, must transcend convenience, break custom, and bear suffering. It must be chosen freely, even if it destroys. The lover's loyalty to the beloved mirrored the believer's loyalty to God—absolute, irrational, pure.

By the 18th and 19th centuries, this aesthetic of exalted feeling had become a moral worldview. The Enlightenment had desacralized the cosmos; Romanticism re-sacralized the self. Thinkers like Rousseau and poets like Goethe turned inward, locating divinity in emotion. The modern subject discovered the infinite within personal passion. To love another became not merely a pleasure but a vocation, a way of knowing the self and the world. And fidelity—the constancy of that passion—became the proof of authenticity. To betray was not only to wound another; it was to falsify one's own soul.

The Romantic era also produced its archetypes of ruin: lovers crushed beneath the weight of their own ideals. Anna Karenina, Emma Bovary, Werther, Catherine and Heathcliff—each destroyed by the same belief that love, if true, must be all-consuming. The modern adulterer ceased to be a libertine and became a tragic hero, torn between social duty and emotional truth. Adultery, in these novels, is not the enemy of fidelity but its excessive expression—the demand that love live up to the ideal that marriage can rarely sustain. In this way, Romanticism deepened monogamy even as it destabilized it: it transformed an institution into a drama of conscience.

By the late nineteenth century, the dream of "the one" had fully crystallized. The bourgeois world, with its nuclear families and sentimental domesticity, demanded that love carry the weight once borne by religion and community. The household became the temple, the couple its clergy. Monogamy was now not only a social contract or a moral duty but an existential horizon. To fail at it was to fail at meaning itself.

This transformation gave love unprecedented dignity. For the first time in history, ordinary people could expect their unions to be based on affection rather than arrangement, on personal choice rather than parental command. Yet the same revolution also set a trap. If marriage was now grounded in emotion, what happened when emotion faded? When God withdrew, divorce was blasphemy; when feeling became sacred, disappointment became despair. The ideal of "the one" turned love into an all-or-nothing wager: either total fulfillment or failure.

The philosopher Denis de Rougemont, in his classic *Love in the Western World*, called this the "passion for passion." The West, he argued, learned to prefer love's intensity to its endurance—to seek ecstasy even at the cost of peace. We inherited from the troubadours and the Romantics a strange moral hierarchy in which suffering proves sincerity. The faithful lover is not the one who stays but the one who feels the most deeply. Hence the paradox of our time: we revere lifelong commitment yet romanticize the affair. Both are children of the same ideal—that love should redeem us from ordinariness.

The modern cult of "the one" thus fuses the religious and the erotic, the sacred and the psychological. It asks two people to do what once took an entire community: to provide each other with meaning, identity, and transcendence. Under such pressure, desire trembles. Fidelity becomes an act of worship, and betrayal, when it occurs, feels like heresy. We continue to live within this theology of the heart, even when we no longer believe in any other god.

The result is the condition of modern love: we expect from another person the eternity that our ancestors once expected from God. Every vow of monogamy now carries the echo of that impossible aspiration—the hope that two finite beings can offer each other something infinite. We keep returning to the altar, knowing that the altar is fragile, and we call this faith.

The Bourgeois Family and the Politics of Fidelity

By the mid-nineteenth century, the dream of Romantic love had settled into the architecture of bourgeois society. What had begun as rebellion — the free choice of love over arrangement — became the moral foundation of the new industrial order. Marriage now promised not only affection but respectability; fidelity was no longer simply a personal virtue, but a civic one. In the emerging middle classes of Europe and America, domestic order mirrored social order: each household a miniature state, ruled by discipline, propriety, and self-control. The home became a moral factory for producing responsible citizens.

The bourgeois family was thus both an emotional haven and a political instrument. In a world of factories and markets, it offered stability amid flux. It tamed male desire and anchored female dependence. The husband's fidelity symbolized self-mastery; the wife's, moral purity. Together, they formed a closed circuit of virtue that justified the broader hierarchies of capitalism and patriarchy. Monogamy, once an aristocratic ornament or a religious command, became the cornerstone of bourgeois respectability — proof that one belonged to the moral middle.

But this order depended on illusion. The same society that preached chastity built an economy of temptation around it. The city, with its anonymity and spectacle, became a stage for duplicity. Behind the façade of domestic virtue thrived a vast shadow economy of desire: brothels, mistresses, courtesans, and pornography. Respectable men could indulge their instincts as long as they did so discreetly, while women were punished for the same transgressions with social death. The "fallen woman" became a stock character of nineteenth-century literature not because she was rare, but because she was necessary — the moral scapegoat who absorbed the sins of the system.

This hypocrisy was not incidental; it was structural. Bourgeois morality required the appearance of restraint, not its reality. The repression of female sexuality sustained male power, and the sanctity of the home depended on the invisibility of everything that occurred outside it. The ideal of the faithful wife was maintained by the availability of women who could not afford to be wives at all. The same double standard echoed through law and custom: adultery by a husband was a misstep, by a wife, a crime.

The philosopher Friedrich Engels, observing Victorian England, called marriage "the domestic enslavement of the woman." Yet even as socialism and feminism began to challenge the material basis of this arrangement, its moral grammar persisted. To be "respectable" still meant to be married, to be sexually contained, to perform the theater of fidelity even when the script rang hollow. Monogamy became the badge of order in a society terrified of disorder — of revolution, of class mixing, of female autonomy.

The household, too, was reimagined as a private fortress of virtue. The poet Coventry Patmore's 1854 poem *The Angel in the House* captured the prevailing fantasy: the wife as moral guardian, self-effacing and pure, her devotion redeeming her husband's worldly sins. But the angel's light cast a long shadow. The ideal left women spiritually exalted yet economically confined, charged with maintaining the very virtue that limited them. It also left men emotionally stunted, trained to find excitement outside the home while treating domestic life as a sanctuary from their own desires.

This gendered choreography of repression and indulgence laid the groundwork for modern alienation. The more monogamy became entwined with virtue, the more it demanded secrecy to survive. The faithful man was not the one who resisted temptation, but the one who managed his transgressions discreetly. Thus, the private hypocrisy that had once characterized kings and courtiers trickled down into the moral life of the clerk and shopkeeper. Respectability depended not on honesty but on silence.

Even today, traces of this legacy persist. The vocabulary of "cheating" and "scandal" still carries the accents of Victorian shame; the sentimental ideal of the nuclear family still borrows its emotional grammar from the domestic novels of the 19th century. The moral code that once disciplined the bourgeoisie now governs the inner lives of the middle classes across the world. What began as a structure for managing property and passion has hardened into a reflex of identity: we still equate fidelity with goodness, not because it always produces happiness, but because it signifies control.

In this sense, the bourgeois family perfected the politics of monogamy. It took an institution born from necessity, purified by religion, and infused with romantic feeling — and turned it into ideology. It taught generations to equate virtue with self-restraint, and to treat deviation not as complexity but as corruption. Yet the tension that sustained this system — between what it demanded and what human beings could deliver — never disappeared. It merely went underground, re-emerging in the art and psychology of the modern age as the recurring theme of spiritual fatigue, marital malaise, and the desperate search for "authenticity" in love.

Once fidelity became the symbol of moral worth, its failure became the modern tragedy par excellence — the wound through which the inner life first began to speak.

The Invention of Romantic Failure

Every civilization has its preferred tragedy. For the ancients, it was hubris: the mortal who defied the gods. For the modern West, it is adultery. The fall from grace that once unfolded on Olympus now occurs in the bedroom. We may live in a secular age, but we continue to stage our moral dramas in the language of love.

By the late nineteenth century, the bourgeois family had become so dominant, and the Romantic ideal of "the one" so absolute, that failure was inevitable. What had once been the moral order of society became the existential order of the self. Love was no longer something that happened within life; it was supposed to *be* life itself — its meaning, its redemption, its proof that we were capable of transcendence. When that promise faltered, the collapse felt cosmic. The adulterer replaced the sinner, and heartbreak replaced damnation.

The great novels of modernity chronicled this fall with forensic precision. Flaubert's Emma Bovary, seduced not by lust but by the idea of romance itself, finds that the dream of perfect passion dissolves into debt, gossip, and despair. Tolstoy's Anna Karenina, trapped between the sanctity of marriage and the intoxication of freedom, discovers that society will forgive hypocrisy but not honesty. In both stories, infidelity is not mere weakness; it is protest — a rebellion against the smallness of life under the weight of an impossible ideal. The lovers' ruin becomes proof of the ideal's power.

These tales taught modern readers something unprecedented: that the failure of love could be as meaningful as its fulfillment. The tragic adulteress became a vessel for moral reflection, a symbol of how desire and virtue tear at each other. Even as audiences condemned her, they also envied her intensity. In a world grown bureaucratic and disenchanted, she embodied the longing to feel absolutely.

The new art forms of the twentieth century extended this aesthetic of failure. In film, David Lean's *Brief Encounter* and Wong Kar-wai's *In the Mood for Love* turned restraint itself into eroticism; longing replaced consummation as the measure of depth. The twentieth-century affair became quieter, more internal — an emotional event rather than a social scandal. Psychoanalysis, meanwhile, recast infidelity as symptom: not sin or heroism, but the expression of unmet needs, repressed fantasies, and the eternal return of the unconscious. What religion had called temptation, Freud called displacement.

Through these transformations, our culture learned to aestheticize disappointment. We built entire industries around it — literature, cinema, therapy. The endless post-mortem of failed relationships became a way of defining identity: "Tell me about your heartbreak" replaced "Tell me about your faith." Even those who claim to despise the adulterer remain fascinated by the possibility that desire might still break through the routines of respectability. We are a civilization of voyeurs, moralizing and yearning in the same breath.

Romantic failure endures because it mirrors our condition. The modern subject is asked to find in one person what previous centuries sought in God and society: meaning, belonging, transcendence, renewal. It is a beautiful demand, and a cruel one. No single human can bear it. The disillusionment that follows is not proof that love is false, but that our expectations have become metaphysical. We do not merely want companionship; we want salvation.

In this light, infidelity and disappointment are not deviations from the story of monogamy; they are its logical conclusion. When fidelity becomes a creed, doubt becomes its sacrament. We betray not because we reject love, but because we cannot stop testing its limits. We fail, and in failing, we discover that our longing is larger than the rules meant to contain it.

That, finally, is the paradox at the heart of modern intimacy: we romanticize fidelity and we romanticize its collapse, worshipping both the altar and the ruins. The great writers understood this long before psychology did: that to be human is to oscillate between devotion and flight, to build meaning from the very fractures we mourn.

Monogamy's invention, then, was not only the creation of an institution but of an aesthetic — the art of loving earnestly enough to suffer for it. We have inherited both the discipline and the discontent. Our faith in love remains, even when we no longer believe in the forms that promise to protect it.

The Persistence of the Vow

Every human order outlives its justification. Monogamy began as a contract, became a commandment, and finally turned into a confession — from property to piety to psychology. Yet through every metamorphosis, the vow has endured. We have changed the gods, but we keep the ritual.

This endurance is not mere habit. Beneath all the hypocrisy and heartbreak lies a stubborn truth: the desire to bind oneself to another, to make permanence out of impermanence, remains one of the deepest expressions of the human spirit. Fidelity survives not because it is easy or natural, but because it is difficult — because it turns instinct into discipline and contingency into meaning. We return to the promise not because it has never failed us, but because it keeps teaching us what it means to begin again.

Monogamy may be an invention, but it is an invention that civilizes desire. Its very impossibility gives it value: it is the form through which we test our capacity for care, patience, and moral imagination. The point is not that we succeed, but that we continue to try.

And yet, as the next chapter will argue, this persistence demands explanation. Why, in an age of freedom and pluralism, when every tradition has been questioned, does monogamy still command our loyalty? What does it give us that other arrangements cannot? And can its meaning be salvaged without the illusions that once sustained it?

These questions lead us forward — from history to philosophy, from the genealogy of fidelity to its justification.

Chapter 3:
Why Monogamy Still Matters

The Ethics of Depth: Love as Practice, Not Feeling

Modern love suffers from a crisis of expectation. We have inherited from Romanticism the belief that love should be spontaneous, effortless, and perpetually self-renewing — that to love truly is to feel endlessly. We imagine the perfect relationship as an unbroken harmony of desire and devotion, a perpetual astonishment sustained without effort. When this fantasy falters, as it must, we interpret its decay as failure. Yet perhaps it is not love that fails, but our idea of it.

Monogamy, at its best, exposes this misconception. It insists that love is not an emotion but a craft — not something we fall into, but something we learn to build. The philosopher Erich Fromm, in *The Art of Loving*, argued that love must be treated like any other discipline: it requires knowledge, patience, concentration, and humility. We do not expect to master music or medicine by intuition alone, yet we assume that affection will sustain itself without training. The truth is that lasting intimacy demands effort, and fidelity is one of its forms.

To commit to one person over time is to consent to the slow work of understanding — to discover, through repetition, that affection is not the enemy of intensity. The daily gestures of care, the small renunciations of pride, the moments of restraint — these are not romantic in the cinematic sense, but they create the texture of trust from which deeper desire can emerge. Monogamy's real virtue lies here, in the transformation of feeling into form. It gives love a body — an architecture through which it can survive its own moods.

The moral philosophers of antiquity would have understood this. Aristotle, in the *Nicomachean Ethics*, distinguished between pleasure, utility, and virtue as the three grounds of friendship. Only the last — *philia* — is stable, because it rests on shared character and purpose rather than on passion or gain. Such friendship, he wrote, requires time: "For as the proverb says, men cannot know each other until they have eaten salt together." Love that endures becomes ethical not because it suppresses passion but because it converts it into the patience of recognition.

In this sense, fidelity is not merely about sexual exclusivity; it is the practice of staying. It is the refusal to treat love as consumption, the willingness to remain present when the novelty fades and the other becomes real. To stay is to bear witness to another person's becoming — to remain long enough for them to change, and to be changed by them in return. This is why the philosopher Simone Weil, writing about attention as the highest form of love, described it as "suspending one's thought, leaving it detached, empty, and ready to receive." In monogamy, such attention becomes an ethic: the discipline of seeing the familiar anew.

Our culture confuses this endurance with stagnation. It treats repetition as death to desire. But repetition, rightly understood, is what allows desire to mature. In music, the refrain gives meaning to variation; in love, constancy gives weight to change. The thrill of a new encounter is easy; the miracle is to find newness within the known. Monogamy's challenge is not to keep feeling what we felt at the beginning, but to keep *discovering* what we could not have known then.

None of this makes fidelity easy. It is a task, not a gift — and precisely for that reason, it is a moral achievement. To stay when departure would be simpler, to tend what time corrodes, to wrestle with boredom and still choose tenderness — these are acts of will that elevate love from instinct to art. The Romantic imagination equated love with intensity; the ethical imagination must learn to equate it with depth.

Monogamy, understood this way, is not a sentimental relic but a school of character. It teaches patience in an age of distraction, humility in an age of narcissism, and steadiness in an age of flux. Its beauty lies not in purity but in practice — in the quiet heroism of two people who, knowing full well the difficulty, decide to stay and make something durable together.

The Politics of Equality: Monogamy and Mutual Recognition

Every love story is also a story about power. Desire rarely exists in a vacuum; it is shaped by hierarchy — of gender, class, and custom. The earliest forms of marriage codified those hierarchies into law: men as owners, women as dependents; fidelity as duty, not as choice. Monogamy, in this original guise, was not a pact between equals but a contract of control. Yet one of the most remarkable moral transformations in human history is that the same structure that once enforced domination became, over centuries, the crucible for equality.

This reversal began when monogamy ceased to be imposed and began to be chosen. Once marriage was no longer primarily an economic alliance or divine commandment, it became a voluntary covenant between two individuals. That voluntariness changed everything. The bond that had once reflected hierarchy could now become the site of reciprocity. To stand before another and promise fidelity freely, without coercion, is to recognize them not as property but as peer — to acknowledge, as the philosopher

G.W.F. Hegel put it, a "mutual recognition" in which each sees the other as a self-conscious being of equal worth.

Hegel believed that love, when genuine, is a dialectic of freedom and unity. Each person must surrender self-centered independence without dissolving into the other. The aim is not domination or submission, but mutual acknowledgment — a relation in which each affirms the other's autonomy precisely by committing to it. In this light, monogamy becomes not a prison of possession but a rehearsal for democracy. It trains the moral imagination to live with another person's freedom without trying to own it.

Historically, this moral promise arrived late. For centuries, men demanded the fidelity they refused to give, and women paid for deviation with ruin. Only with the slow emancipation of women — through literacy, labor, and political rights — did the language of marriage begin to change. Fidelity, once the emblem of obedience, could finally become a sign of equality: two individuals, bound not by law but by mutual consent, vowing exclusivity as an act of shared agency. The double standard that excused male infidelity and condemned female desire exposed itself as the residue of a vanished order.

Modern monogamy, insofar as it is ethical, depends on this symmetry. Its moral core lies not in purity but in reciprocity: the belief that two people owe each other the same measure of honesty, freedom, and restraint. That belief, fragile as it is, carries revolutionary potential. It presumes that intimacy should be governed by fairness, not power — that love itself can be democratic.

This is what distinguishes monogamy, properly understood, from older forms of exclusivity and from some of its contemporary alternatives. Polygyny, historically justified by wealth and patriarchy, multiplies inequality: one man's abundance becomes another's deprivation. In many modern forms of polyamory, meanwhile, the ideal of freedom sometimes collapses into its own asymmetries — emotional labor unevenly distributed, desire rationalized into hierarchy by other means. Monogamy, by contrast, can at least aspire to balance: it limits the field so that equality has space to grow. Two people, bound by the same rules, must continually negotiate the terms of their coexistence. In that negotiation lies the moral work.

The feminist philosopher Carole Pateman once argued that modern marriage, when freely chosen, could symbolize the "sexual contract" as an act of mutual recognition rather than subordination. In practice, this means that fidelity becomes not a mechanism of control but a language of respect. To remain faithful is not to claim ownership but to affirm worth; to stay is to testify that the other's individuality, far from threatening the bond, sustains it.

Of course, this ideal remains unevenly realized. Economic dependency, cultural scripts, and structural power still shape who can afford to choose equality and who must perform it. Yet even in its imperfection, the aspiration itself matters. In a society saturated with transactional relationships — with competition, consumption, and commodified intimacy — monogamy's stubborn insistence on reciprocity stands as a small act of resistance. It reminds us that love, like justice, begins with the recognition of another as an end, not a means.

To share a life under such conditions is to practice democracy in miniature: a continuous, difficult negotiation of freedom and responsibility, of self and other, of the wish to merge and the right to remain distinct. That, more than romance, is what gives monogamy its moral gravity. It trains us for coexistence — for the daily ethics of equality that society too often preaches in public but neglects in private.

The Economics of Attention: Love in the Age of Distraction

Ours is the most distracted civilization in history. Never before have human beings had so many ways to communicate, and so little to say with patience. Every moment is a marketplace of stimuli, every screen a slot machine for desire. We scroll, swipe, and refresh through infinite invitations — each one promising connection, none demanding endurance. The very technologies that were supposed to bring us closer have turned intimacy into a form of consumption.

Within this economy of distraction, monogamy appears at first glance an anachronism, a relic of scarcity in a world of abundance. Why settle, we are told, when the world is infinite and the algorithm never sleeps? Yet this very abundance has hollowed out the conditions for real connection. Choice, once a symbol of freedom, has become a new form of bondage — the tyranny of the possible. Desire now exhausts itself not in possession but in attention, spent across a thousand fragments before it can gather into meaning.

The philosopher Byung-Chul Han, in *The Burnout Society*, calls this the pathology of our age: we no longer inhabit time, we consume it. In a world where everything competes for our attention, depth becomes subversive. To sustain interest in one person, one task, one thought, requires rebellion against the logic of distraction. Monogamy, in this light, is not repression but resistance — a refusal to scatter the self.

Fidelity, then, is not merely sexual exclusivity; it is attentional exclusivity. It is the choice to focus one's psychic energy on a single, evolving relationship, rather than dispersing it across a multitude of fleeting gratifications. This does not mean blindness to beauty elsewhere, but a deliberate act of prioritization: to say, "I will give the best of my awareness to you." In a time when every click and scroll is a micro-infidelity of attention, this is a radical gesture.

The psychoanalyst Jacques Lacan once wrote that "love is giving something you don't have to someone who doesn't want it." Perhaps, in the twenty-first century, what we don't have is focus — the ability to be still, to attend. To love someone faithfully now means to reclaim that scarce resource from the digital marketplace and offer it freely. Monogamy becomes, paradoxically, an ecological practice: the conservation of attention against the endless extraction of desire.

Even within relationships, the contagion of distraction corrodes intimacy. Partners become spectators to each other's curated selves — glancing up from their screens to exchange reports from elsewhere. We outsource desire to fantasy, companionship to devices, conversation to messaging apps. The rituals that once grounded intimacy — eye contact, shared silence, the tactile slowness of affection — struggle to compete with the immediacy of the feed.

Monogamy offers a counterpoint to this dispersal. It reintroduces scarcity where the world offers surplus, and by doing so, makes meaning possible again. Its constraint is what gives it value. The lover who limits his or her field of attention creates the conditions for recognition — for the other person to emerge not as one among many, but as irreplaceable. As the philosopher Iris Murdoch argued, "Love is the extremely difficult realization that something other than oneself is real." Attention, disciplined and sustained, is how that realization takes root.

This is why fidelity feels heavy: it demands that we resist the frictionless economy of distraction and remain present within difficulty. It asks us to turn toward what we might prefer to scroll past — to stay when our instincts call for novelty, to listen when we crave escape. The erotic charge of newness is replaced by the moral charge of care. Both are forms of desire; only one deepens it.

To practice monogamy in this world is to take a stand for duration. It is to reclaim time from the algorithm, to build continuity in a culture of interruption. The faithfulness that once served God or law now serves attention itself — the most endangered faculty of the self. In this sense, fidelity has become a political act: a refusal to let love be dissolved into content.

Our ancestors pledged loyalty to resist chaos; we must now pledge it to resist distraction. The struggle is the same: to hold one thing in mind long enough for it to matter.

The Need for Mystery: Why Desire Requires Boundaries

Every intimacy lives within a paradox: we long for closeness, but we also long for distance. We want to merge completely with the person we love — to be seen, known, and absorbed — yet we also want the thrill of discovery, the electric charge of the unknown. Love seeks unity; desire thrives on difference. Without limits, one dies; without connection, the other starves.

Monogamy, for all its constraints, remains one of the few arrangements that takes this paradox seriously. It offers a structure within which freedom and limit can coexist — where mystery is not abolished but contained, given form. The temptation to dissolve all boundaries in the name of openness misunderstands the nature of erotic life. The problem with complete transparency is not moral but imaginative: it leaves no space for curiosity.

The psychoanalyst Esther Perel captures this tension with rare clarity. "Love," she writes, "thrives on closeness; desire requires distance." The more we know about our partners — their histories, their habits, their flaws — the less room we leave for projection, fantasy, and surprise. The paradox of long-term love is that the same familiarity that nurtures safety also threatens excitement. Desire depends on otherness, even — or especially — in those we know best.

Here, boundaries perform a creative function. They mark off a space where desire can breathe — a space of not-knowing within the known. The faithful relationship that endures is not the one without secrets, but the one that manages them gracefully. It understands that intimacy need not mean total disclosure. A certain opacity — the subtle right to one's inner life — keeps eroticism alive. The self must remain partly foreign if it is to remain alluring.

The philosopher Georg Simmel called this the "secret" as the soul of relationship — not because secrecy is deceitful, but because it preserves individuality. Every bond, he argued, requires a frontier: a point beyond which the other remains sovereign. Without such frontiers, love risks collapsing into sameness, and sameness into indifference. The ethical task is not to abolish the boundary but to maintain it with tenderness.

This is the insight that some modern discourses of "ethical non-monogamy" overlook. They mistake transparency for truth, as if the confession of desire could neutralize its volatility. But desire does not obey management; it thrives in ambiguity. The promise of total openness — that we might domesticate jealousy or control attraction by naming them — often leads to a subtler form of control. What begins as freedom can end as surveillance, every encounter negotiated until spontaneity is exhausted.

Monogamy, by contrast, channels this danger into form. Its limits are not moral prohibitions so much as aesthetic ones — the way a poem's rhyme scheme gives rhythm to its feeling. Fidelity is the meter of love, not its censor. It allows intensity to accumulate rather than disperse. To desire within limits is to deepen rather than diffuse; it is to explore the infinite variations of the finite.

This is not an argument for prudishness, nor for the moral superiority of the "closed" relationship. It is an argument for the creative necessity of form. Just as an artist requires constraint to create beauty, lovers require limits to generate meaning. The refusal of every boundary produces not liberation but entropy: a drift into indifference, where nothing feels forbidden and therefore nothing feels charged.

Mystery, then, is not a residue of repression but the atmosphere of desire. It is what allows two people to remain strange to each other — to keep rediscovering the distance that intimacy slowly erases. The faithful couple who still intrigue one another, who still reserve parts of themselves for silence or surprise, practice a subtler kind of erotic freedom: not the freedom to leave, but the freedom to remain unpredictable within what endures.

In this sense, monogamy does not extinguish desire; it refines it. It teaches that the boundary is not a wall but a mirror — a surface across which two selves learn to see each other anew. Its discipline lies in preserving that shimmer of difference within continuity, that brief flicker of "I do not yet fully know you," even after decades of saying goodnight.

Desire cannot live without boundaries because boundaries give it shape. To surrender entirely is to end the dance; to hold back a little is to keep the music playing.

The Existential Argument: Monogamy as a Human Art of Meaning

Every love story is, in the end, a struggle against time. The body changes, desire fades, memory erodes; everything that once felt infinite reveals its limits. What lovers seek, beneath pleasure or companionship, is a small defiance of this decay — a way to make the passing moment last. Monogamy, in its most serious sense, is not merely a moral choice but an existential one: it is an attempt to give shape to impermanence, to create continuity where nature offers none.

To promise to stay is to rebel against transience. It is to say, *I will make something endure even as the world unravels.* This promise is not naïve; it knows that time will corrode, that love will falter, that neither purity nor certainty is possible. Its beauty lies in the defiance. Every vow of fidelity contains a quiet metaphysical gesture: to take the raw material of contingency — chance encounters, fallible bodies, fragile feelings — and turn them into form.

The philosopher Albert Camus, writing about the artist's task in *The Myth of Sisyphus*, saw meaning as an act of resistance: "The struggle itself toward the heights is enough to fill a man's heart." Fidelity, like art, is this kind of struggle — an act of will against absurdity. We know that love will not save us from time, yet we make it anyway, shaping our days into a pattern of care. The point is not to conquer decay but to make its presence bearable, to carve beauty into the passing.

Monogamy intensifies that difficulty by extending it over years. It demands that we sustain attention not only through novelty but through fatigue, boredom, disappointment, and change. It asks that we recognize the beloved, again and again, through each of their metamorphoses — to keep seeing them as real when familiarity tempts us to abstraction. This continuous act of seeing becomes a moral discipline: the repetition through which compassion acquires depth.

If passion is how love begins, attention is how it survives. And if time is what erodes desire, time is also what gives it dimension. The repetition of fidelity — the mundane cycles of shared life, the rituals that mark passing days — transforms love from event into narrative. It turns feeling into history. To look back and say, *We have lasted,* is to discover a meaning that no single instant could contain.

This, ultimately, is the quiet grandeur of monogamy: it allows two finite beings to make something infinite in duration, if not in scope. It is not eternity, but a rhythm that gestures toward it — a mortal approximation of permanence. Each promise kept becomes a kind of art, a way of shaping chaos into continuity. We build cathedrals of memory out of the ordinary acts of staying.

To love one person through time is not to deny change but to weave it into form. Fidelity does not fix the self or the other in place; it provides a frame in which both may evolve. The true opposite of freedom is not commitment but indifference. The lover who stays does not surrender liberty but redefines it: freedom as constancy, will as care, choice as repetition.

This is why monogamy continues to matter even when its cultural scaffolding has fallen away. It is not an answer to our instincts but an argument with them — a way of transforming biology into ethics, and ethics into art. In choosing to stay, we participate in one of humanity's oldest creative gestures: the making of meaning from impermanence.

And so fidelity endures, not because it is easy or natural, but because it gives us something rarer than pleasure — it gives us *form*. In a world that dissolves everything into flux, that form becomes a kind of salvation: the proof that we can still choose, still bind, still build something that lasts even as we fade.

The Weight and Grace of Staying

To remain faithful is to live inside a contradiction. We promise permanence in a world that promises nothing back. We bind ourselves to another, knowing full well that time will unbind us, that desire will ebb, that memory will distort. Yet this is precisely what gives the promise its weight. Fidelity is not the absence of freedom, but its most deliberate expression — the freedom to return, to repair, to remain.

Every generation rediscovers this truth in its own idiom. We tell ourselves that we are freer, that we have outgrown the vows and limits of the past, and yet we still reach for them — perhaps because love without gravity drifts into sentiment, while love with weight becomes meaning. Monogamy survives not as an inherited rule but as a chosen resistance: an act of coherence in a fragmented world.

Still, even as we honor this endurance, we cannot ignore the tremor beneath it — the restlessness that no vow can still. The same consciousness that builds fidelity also dreams of escape; the same imagination that sustains the home also imagines its undoing. If monogamy is the art of making permanence bearable, infidelity is the art of remembering that we are alive.

The question, then, is not whether the impulse to stray is immoral, but whether it can be understood — even, perhaps, redeemed. Beyond betrayal lies another philosophical question: can the desire to transgress coexist with love, not as its negation but as its shadow?

That question begins the next chapter.

Chapter 4:
Chapter 4: The Limits of Non-Monogamy

———————◄O►————————

The Dream of Infinite Freedom

The modern imagination is haunted by a single promise: that liberation will finally make us whole. We have been taught to believe that constraint is the root of all suffering, that every limit is an injury to authenticity. This conviction has found its most intimate expression in our ideas about love. Where earlier generations sought stability, ours seeks expansion. Fidelity, once the measure of virtue, now risks appearing as fear. The highest good, we are told, is honesty — and the purest honesty is openness.

From this belief has emerged an ethic that treats exclusivity as an anachronism. The new romantic ideal is flexibility: arrangements without ownership, transparency without obligation, pleasure without shame. We speak of *ethical non-monogamy*, *relationship anarchy*, *conscious polyamory* — each phrase attempting to rescue desire from repression by moralizing its multiplicity. The vocabulary is that of progress: to love many is to evolve beyond scarcity, to transcend the jealous economies of the past.

It is easy to see the appeal. Monogamy, with its long history of hypocrisy and gendered injustice, has earned its critics. The promise of openness speaks to a genuine hunger — the wish to be truthful about attraction, to live without deceit, to honor the complexity of the heart rather than police it. It imagines love as abundance rather than confinement. At its most generous, it proposes that affection need not be zero-sum: that intimacy, like light, multiplies when shared.

Yet beneath this utopian vocabulary lies a subtler exhaustion. The same culture that preaches freedom also produces anxiety: endless negotiation, emotional bookkeeping, the fatigue of constant self-disclosure. In place of repression, we invent bureaucracy; in place of silence, the obligation to explain. Desire, once a mystery, becomes a meeting agenda. The pursuit of absolute openness risks replacing guilt with exhaustion — the moral duty to process every impulse, to map every contour of one's desire.

The philosopher Zygmunt Bauman called this condition *liquid love*: relationships that aspire to depth but fear duration, forever flexible yet never secure. In a world where everything is provisional — jobs, cities, identities — love too becomes a temporary contract, renewed at each moment by mutual convenience. What appears as freedom often conceals its opposite: the terror of dependency, the refusal to risk permanence. We float from encounter to encounter, mistaking motion for vitality.

Nietzsche, in a different context, warned that liberation is not an end but a beginning: "Freedom from something is only the first step; freedom for something is the next." The trouble with much of our contemporary openness is that it stops at the first step. It frees us from constraint but gives us no telos, no shared direction. The self becomes an open system with no coherence, forever exploring but rarely belonging. In the realm of love, this yields a peculiar melancholy: we are surrounded by possibilities, yet starving for meaning.

What the rhetoric of infinite freedom forgets is that choice, without form, corrodes desire. When everything is permitted, nothing feels precious. The thrill of transgression depends on the existence of a border; remove the border, and excitement flattens into indifference. Monogamy's constraint, for all its burdens, at least gives passion a shape — a horizon against which longing can unfold. Freedom without resistance becomes another kind of monotony, an ocean without shore.

This is not to condemn openness, but to recognize its tragic dimension. Human beings need both air and gravity. The attempt to abolish limits entirely often ends not in ecstasy but in fatigue — the weariness of constant self-reinvention. The dream of infinite freedom, when pursued without structure, leads not to expansion but to dispersion. What begins as liberation ends as drift.

The next section explores the moral logic that sustains this drift: the belief that complete transparency can replace trust. But as we shall see, the promise of openness is haunted by its own paradox — that in trying to eliminate secrecy, we extinguish the very mystery that makes love worth telling the truth about.

The Myth of Transparency

If the modern faith in freedom has a sacrament, it is confession. We live in an age that believes truth should always be spoken, that withholding is a kind of betrayal, and that transparency will save us from misunderstanding. The ideal relationship, in this moral economy, is one without opacity: every feeling named, every attraction declared, every past desire accounted for. The highest virtue is disclosure.

This ethic of transparency animates much of contemporary non-monogamy. The logic runs like this: if secrecy destroys trust, then honesty must heal it. If infidelity lies, then openness must tell the truth. By exposing every desire to light, we imagine we will dissolve the shadow of jealousy. But desire is not a bureaucracy that yields to audit. Its power lies precisely in what escapes articulation.

The philosopher Michel Foucault, writing about the "confessional society," warned that the modern compulsion to speak—about sex, about the self—produces not liberation but new forms of discipline. To confess everything is to internalize surveillance; to catalogue desire is to turn passion into paperwork. We no longer hide what we feel, but we monitor it endlessly. Love becomes a performance of sincerity, measured in disclosures per minute.

The paradox is that transparency, pursued to its limit, destroys intimacy. To be fully known is to lose the space in which curiosity can live. The mystery that sustains desire—the small, sacred unknown in which imagination thrives—evaporates under the glare of constant revelation. The more we tell, the less there is to discover. The couple who prides themselves on "absolute honesty" risk becoming archivists of their own disillusionment.

Psychoanalysis teaches a humbler truth: that much of what we feel cannot be confessed because it is not fully known even to ourselves. The unconscious resists management; it speaks in slips and silences. To make transparency the supreme virtue is to demand from love an impossible clarity, to turn the other into an interpreter rather than a companion. The question "What are you feeling?" can become a weapon of control disguised as care.

There is, instead, a gentler ethic—one that values discretion without deceit. Every intimacy requires boundaries between what can be shared and what must remain unspoken, not out of shame but out of reverence. Recall how Georg Simmel once wrote that the secret is the soul of relationship because it preserves individuality. To protect a secret is not to lie; it is to keep alive the part of the self that cannot be absorbed by another. Love needs that remainder, the inner country that no one else can occupy.

In this light, monogamy's old reticence—its modesty, its silences—need not be read only as repression. It can also be read as a kind of tact, an acknowledgment that total visibility annihilates the erotic. When everything is shared, nothing is sacred. The ethical task, then, is not to abolish secrecy but to make it humane: to distinguish concealment that protects tenderness from concealment that deceives.

Transparency imagines that honesty is enough; in truth, love demands something harder—trust. To trust is to live without complete knowledge, to accept the other's opacity as part of their dignity. It is to replace surveillance with faith, to exchange confession for confidence. This is the paradox that modern liberation has forgotten: that intimacy depends not on knowing everything, but on believing that there are things we do not need to know.

To love, in this sense, is to let the other remain partly mysterious—and to find in that mystery not threat, but grace.

The Economics of Desire

Modern desire speaks the language of the market. We swipe, select, match, upgrade, exit. Every romantic encounter is mediated by the logic of choice, by the same interface that sells us everything else. The apps and platforms that promise intimacy are built on the same code as the ones that deliver groceries or flights: algorithms of comparison. We no longer fall in love; we optimize for it.

This economy of desire has reshaped how we imagine freedom. To be liberated is to have options. The mark of oppression is scarcity; the mark of progress, abundance. In this calculus, the monogamous couple appears as an inefficient monopoly, while the polyamorous subject becomes a diversified portfolio. "Ethical non-monogamy" borrows not only the moral language of sincerity, but also the managerial language of flexibility, openness, and growth. Partners are reimagined as nodes in a network, desire as renewable energy.

But the market's logic is insatiable. It transforms every experience into potential for more. Where the sacred once limited, the market expands. The promise of polyamory—that love, like knowledge, grows by sharing—too easily mirrors the promise of capitalism: that limitless circulation yields limitless fulfillment. Both rest on the same illusion—that expansion can substitute for depth, and novelty for meaning.

The sociologist Eva Illouz, in *Consuming the Romantic Utopia*, observed that modern relationships are structured by the grammar of consumerism. We learn to equate choice with self-expression, and passion with intensity. The more options we have, the more we fear missing out; the more we compare, the more we doubt. Even freedom begins to feel like labor — the endless work of selecting, negotiating, and optimizing ourselves for others.

In this marketplace of the heart, even ethics becomes transactional. We speak of "emotional labor," "negotiated boundaries," "relationship agreements" — as if love were a contract between consultants. The language of care is bureaucratized; every feeling requires documentation. What began as an attempt to dignify communication risks turning intimacy into administration.

This managerial vision of love breeds a new anxiety: the fear of inefficiency. To be devoted to one person seems indulgent, even uneconomic — a poor return on emotional investment. Monogamy becomes the emotional equivalent of "buying local": quaint, restrictive, morally suspicious. And yet, the same people who pursue infinite choice often confess exhaustion. The constant openness demanded by the market of desire is indistinguishable from loneliness.

The anthropologist David Graeber once wrote that capitalism's deepest promise is not wealth but imagination — the fantasy that life could always be otherwise. In this sense, polyamory is capitalism's erotic mirror: it turns longing into an infinite horizon, desire into an endless project. The problem is not multiplicity itself but its logic — the belief that the self can expand indefinitely without cost. We pursue experiences not because they satisfy, but because they defer the moment of reckoning with finitude.

Monogamy, by contrast, forces a confrontation with limits. It denies the fantasy of infinite expansion and demands the harder freedom of depth: the freedom to choose one path and live with its consequences. In a culture that prizes flexibility above all else, that is a countercultural act. To stay is to resist not only temptation, but the market's command to keep moving.

None of this is to suggest that non-monogamy cannot contain genuine love, or that monogamy is immune to commodification. The point is that the modern economy of desire colonizes both. It replaces eros — the movement toward what is good and beautiful — with appetite, the movement toward what is new. We confuse circulation for vitality, and in doing so, we cheapen both.

The most radical gesture, then, may no longer be to open every door, but to close one deliberately. To say *enough* in a culture that mistakes restlessness for freedom is to reclaim desire from the market's restless grammar. In that refusal — that quiet "no" to infinite choice — begins the possibility of love as something more than transaction: as attention, as form, as care.

The Moral Psychology of Infidelity

Few acts generate more moral heat than infidelity. To betray is to cross a boundary sanctified by trust, to wound the other's faith in the permanence of love. Yet to understand why people cheat, one must first admit that the act is rarely simple. It is not only lust that drives transgression, but loneliness, curiosity, resentment, the hunger to feel alive again. Betrayal, in this sense, is both a moral failure and a human confession: an admission that the life one is living no longer feels large enough.

The theologian Paul Tillich once defined sin as "separation." In this light, adultery is the symptom of a separation that already exists — a fracture not necessarily between two bodies, but within the self. The adulterer seeks reconciliation with a lost part of themselves: the self before responsibility, before routine, before predictability. They are not always escaping their partner; they are escaping the person they have become.

In moral terms, this makes infidelity tragic rather than merely corrupt. It reveals the conflict between two legitimate goods: truth and vitality, constancy and freedom. Kierkegaard, reflecting on Abraham's willingness to sacrifice Isaac, called this kind of conflict the "teleological suspension of the ethical": a moment when duty to the universal (in this case, the moral law of fidelity) is suspended in obedience to a higher, private necessity. The adulterer, like Abraham, believes that they are obeying something sacred within — not God, perhaps, but the call of authenticity.

But authenticity, pursued at the expense of others, becomes solipsism. The line between the courageous and the cruel is vanishingly thin. The philosopher Ayn Rand, for all her moral eccentricities, grasped one part of this paradox: she defended selfishness as a form of honesty, but her mistake was to forget that love, too, is a form of truth. To seek one's own fulfillment at the cost of another's humiliation is not liberation; it is vanity.

Still, not every act of infidelity is purely destructive. Sometimes, transgression reveals what complacency concealed. The illicit affair may expose how a marriage has calcified into habit, how silence has replaced speech, how desire has been domesticated into duty. In this sense, cheating can serve as a mirror held up to love's decay — an ugly, undeniable proof that the relationship's moral order no longer fits its emotional reality. The question, then, is not whether transgression should occur, but what one does with what it reveals.

There is a difference between the *libertine* and the *penitent*. The libertine seeks conquest; the penitent seeks understanding. The first betrays to escape; the second betrays to know. The ethical adulterer — if such a figure exists — is one who refuses self-deception: who recognizes their act as both rebellion and failure, and who takes responsibility for its consequences without retreating into cynicism. In their turmoil lies a strange kind of moral intelligence — a recognition that fidelity and desire are not enemies, but dialectical partners in the same drama of freedom.

From this perspective, the "crime" of infidelity is not only that it breaks trust, but that it unmasks us. It reveals how much of our moral life depends on performance: the roles of lover, spouse, parent, citizen. To cheat is to interrupt that script and discover, for a moment, the raw contingency beneath it. The exhilaration of the affair often comes less from pleasure than from the temporary collapse of meaning — a vertigo of freedom in which everything feels possible again.

But that freedom is short-lived. What follows is not triumph but interpretation: the search to make sense of what has been done. This is where infidelity returns to ethics. Its aftermath forces a reckoning — not only with one's partner, but with oneself. It asks: what did I hope to find? What did I risk losing? Do I regret the act, or the necessity that drove it? These are not questions that moral prohibitions can answer; they belong to conscience, that uneasy frontier between freedom and guilt.

In a strange way, this is why adultery endures in art and literature: it dramatizes the soul's encounter with its own ambiguity. It is where passion meets conscience, where freedom tests its limits, where love reveals itself as a moral practice rather than a feeling. In that collision lies both devastation and insight.

The task is not to romanticize infidelity, but to understand it as part of love's vocabulary — the word spoken when silence has become unbearable. What matters is not the transgression itself, but whether it deepens one's capacity for truth. To stray and return wiser may be a higher form of fidelity than to stay and forget why.

The Erotics of Constraint

Every age tells itself that it has liberated desire. And every age, sooner or later, rediscovers that desire depends on what resists it. Eros is not the energy of freedom alone, but of friction — of what cannot be had, what must be waited for, what must be imagined. In love, as in art, form gives feeling its pulse. The rule is not an enemy of intensity; it is its condition.

Freud, in *Civilization and Its Discontents*, argued that repression is the price of culture — that without constraint, libido diffuses into aimlessness. It is the wall that gives the mural shape. What psychoanalysis adds to moral philosophy is the recognition that prohibition is not merely external. The "no" that generates desire is internalized; it becomes part of the psyche's architecture. To abolish repression altogether is to abolish eros itself, for desire without resistance loses its object.

Our cultural fantasies understand this instinctively. Consider Don Draper in *Mad Men*: a man who can have almost anyone, yet whose very abundance of choice corrodes meaning. His serial infidelities are not acts of freedom but symptoms of fatigue; what he truly longs for is not conquest, but the lost excitement of transgression — the tension that only constraint could provide. His affairs burn brightly because they are forbidden; once they become permitted, they dissolve.

Or take Tony Soprano, whose affairs are never only about sex, but about sovereignty. The thrill lies not in pleasure but in secrecy — in the gap between who he is and who he pretends to be. His duplicity is what gives his life texture. He senses, dimly, that the moral order he violates is the very one that sustains him; without it, he would be nothing but appetite. That is the paradox of the modern libertine: his rebellion requires the cage he despises.

Scenes from a Marriage, in both Bergman's original and the modern remake, offers the inverse perspective: two people who have already torn down the walls of convention, only to find that freedom brings no peace. Their estrangement is not caused by repression but by its absence. When everything is permitted, nothing feels necessary. What once burned with secrecy now cools into transparency. The lovers discover that even pain had purpose when it was bounded by promise.

These fictions do not moralize so much as diagnose. They understand that constraint is not merely social but erotic: it preserves tension, distance, and imagination. The forbidden glance, the restrained touch, the word left unsaid — these are the choreography of desire. The more easily we can have something, the less we feel its pull. The pleasure of longing lies precisely in its incompleteness.

In this sense, monogamy's prohibitions perform a paradoxical service. They turn the ordinary into the charged, the everyday into the exceptional. Within its boundaries, each act of desire regains its gravity. To choose one person again and again is to re-enchant the familiar, to make repetition erotic through devotion. The same limit that frustrates also intensifies: by forbidding everything, it makes what is allowed luminous.

The allure of the affair, then, is not proof that monogamy is obsolete, but that it works. The boundary holds precisely because it can be broken — and in that tension, desire endures. To abolish limits in the name of honesty or freedom is to flatten this dialectic; to preserve them, even while acknowledging their fragility, is to keep the erotic alive.

Constraint, when freely chosen, is not repression but rhythm. It transforms instinct into form, chaos into music. The lovers who remain faithful not because they must, but because they have decided to, inhabit a subtler kind of erotic life — one that derives its fire not from rebellion but from recurrence.

65

In this light, the moralists and the libertines are both half right. The moralist sees that unbounded desire destroys itself; the libertine sees that repression can become cruelty. But between these extremes lies a third possibility: the art of voluntary limitation. To live within form without losing intensity — that is the true achievement of eros.

The next section turns from this aesthetic paradox to its moral resolution. If transgression is inevitable, can return be redemptive? Can one wander and still remain faithful, not to a rule but to a meaning? In that question — the possibility of falling without forsaking — lies the ethics of what we might call *ethical infidelity*.

The Ethics of Return

Every moral life is measured not by its avoidance of error, but by its capacity for recovery. To love is to expose oneself to failure — of courage, of imagination, of endurance. The point is not to never fall, but to return differently. Fidelity, in this broader sense, is not the absence of betrayal; it is the art of reconciliation.

In religious language, this would be called repentance. But outside theology, repentance need not mean self-abasement. It can mean *understanding* — the willingness to confront the truth of what one has done and to transform it into knowledge. The unfaithful partner who refuses denial, who faces the wound they have caused and the emptiness that led them there, enacts a moral labor more profound than the one who has never been tested. To break and rebuild, if done sincerely, is a higher form of keeping faith.

Camus called revolt "the certainty of a crushing fate, without the resignation that should accompany it." In the context of love, revolt means refusing to let failure have the last word. It means affirming that the broken bond can still bear meaning, that love's value does not vanish with its purity. To stray and return wiser is to reaffirm, against the cynicism of the age, that love is still worth the risk of ruin.

This is why forgiveness, though it may seem sentimental, is one of the most radical acts in human life. It breaks the cycle of transaction — of guilt and punishment — and replaces it with the economy of grace. To forgive is not to excuse, but to recognize that imperfection is the common language of intimacy. It is to love someone for the limits of their freedom as much as for its expression.

The faithful relationship that endures betrayal does not restore innocence; it creates something new. Its trust is not the naïveté of the beginning, but the hard-won clarity of having faced the abyss together. What remains afterward is not purity, but depth — the knowledge that love can survive its own contradiction.

We are accustomed to thinking of infidelity as the opposite of fidelity, but perhaps they are not opposites at all. They are, rather, points on a single curve — one testing the strength of the other. Without the possibility of straying, fidelity would be meaningless; without the possibility of return, betrayal would be irredeemable. The moral work of love lies in moving between these poles without despair.

There is an ancient wisdom in this rhythm. In the Book of Hosea, God commands the prophet to love a faithless woman as a parable of divine fidelity. The lesson is not that betrayal is holy, but that love is larger than betrayal. The same pattern recurs in secular form throughout art and literature: the wanderer who comes home changed, the adulterer who discovers that the very act of transgression has deepened their understanding of devotion. What survives is not the perfection of purity, but the persistence of care.

To return, then, is not to undo the past but to accept it — to make peace with the fragments and carry them forward. The moral beauty of love lies not in its innocence but in its endurance: its ability to outlast shame, to survive its own collapse, to rebuild meaning from the rubble of contradiction.

67

In this way, infidelity can become ethical — not because it is justified, but because it can lead to insight. It teaches humility, exposes illusion, restores gratitude. It reminds us that to love truly is to forgive both the other and oneself for being human.

After the Fall

All freedom ends in form. We learn this slowly, through longing and mistake. We push against the walls that hold us, only to discover that without walls, we lose the shape of our desire. The same discovery repeats itself in every generation, every affair, every confession: the realization that love without boundaries dissolves, and boundaries without love suffocate. Between the two lies the narrow passage of the human heart.

Infidelity, in this light, is not the antithesis of fidelity but its dark tutor. It exposes what our virtues conceal: that the hunger for freedom and the need for belonging are not enemies, but twins forever at war. To betray is to learn how fragile goodness is; to forgive is to learn that it can still endure. What matters, finally, is not whether one has transgressed, but whether one has returned with clearer eyes.

But return does not end the story. To have seen the abyss is to live with its memory. Many who glimpse that void — who feel, however briefly, the vertigo of absolute freedom — do not come back whole. They carry an ache that domestic peace cannot quiet. For some, that ache becomes a restless search for substitutes: the next thrill, the next distraction, the next chance to feel alive. When love is restored, meaning may still be missing.

This, too, is part of the human pattern, and nowhere more visible than in the lives of men. Having been taught that desire is conquest and control, many men cannot bear the stillness that follows forgiveness. Their rebellion turns inward, mutating into addiction, fantasy, or despair. What begins as a search for vitality ends as an exhaustion of the self.

The next chapter turns to this landscape of substitution —
the economy of modern escapisms in which men lose and
sometimes rediscover themselves. It asks why the hunger for risk,
once a force of creation, so easily curdles into destruction; why the
same impulse that drives invention also drives ruin; and whether
there exists a more honest outlet for that restlessness — a way to
seek release without disintegration.

Chapter 5:
Escapism and the Male Impulse

The Anatomy of Escape

Every man has a room he cannot sit quietly in. That room may be his marriage, his office, his car, or his own mind — but the condition is the same. He cannot bear stillness. The modern man's tragedy is not that he lacks pleasure, but that pleasure no longer relieves him. His life is full, yet hollowed out by a constant hum of dissatisfaction — the background noise of a nervous system built for danger now stranded in comfort.

No scene captures this condition better than Tony Soprano slouched in Dr. Melfi's chair. A mob boss with an empire at his command, Tony finds himself weeping without understanding why. His body betrays him: panic attacks, shortness of breath, the sudden collapse of composure. The violence that sustains him in one world offers no power in another. In the silence of therapy, stripped of action, he discovers the true terror of modern masculinity — impotence not of the body but of the soul.

Tony's predicament is not unique. He is the modern everyman, caught between power and purposelessness. He cheats, drinks, eats, and kills not only out of appetite but out of anesthesia — to drown the hum of meaninglessness. His excesses are not celebrations of freedom but symptoms of captivity: the inability to live without stimulation, the fear that without chaos he will disappear. The mobster's existential problem is the suburban man's, only amplified — both are haunted by the question: *what now?*

This hunger for escape has ancient roots. Biologically, men are creatures of pursuit. Evolution wired their reward systems for risk and novelty. Testosterone, dopamine, and adrenaline conspire to make challenge feel like oxygen. For millennia, this chemistry served a purpose: to hunt, to protect, to build, to conquer. But in a world where physical danger has been outsourced and existential danger repressed, those circuits have nowhere to go. The hunt survives only as simulation.

So men invent dangers: the high-speed car, the bar fight, the bet, the affair. Each promises the same surge of aliveness once provoked by survival itself. But these modern substitutes differ in one crucial way — they produce risk without meaning. The hunter once sought food; the gambler seeks chance for its own sake. Pleasure replaces purpose. The problem is not that men chase sensation, but that the chase no longer connects to anything larger than the self.

This is why escapism feels at once thrilling and empty. It mimics transcendence without delivering it. The drinker mistakes intoxication for release; the porn addict confuses stimulus for connection; the workaholic imagines control as significance. Each is a parody of a lost ritual — the ritual of transformation. Once, men entered danger to prove courage, to test limits, to serve a cause. Now they enter it only to feel briefly real.

The psychologist Viktor Frankl wrote that when meaning collapses, pleasure and power rush in to fill the void. The result is the pathology of our age: men drowning in abundance, desperate for the friction of constraint. They long for a struggle that would justify their strength — a difficulty worthy of their restlessness. In its absence, they become consumers of their own disquiet, endlessly medicating the symptom rather than naming the wound.

At its core, escapism is not about pleasure but avoidance — a refusal to confront the unbearable lightness of being unneeded. The man who drinks or gambles or cheats is not always trying to destroy himself; he is trying to *find* himself, to restore the lost correspondence between effort and meaning. But when his escape offers no revelation, only relief, it deepens the alienation it sought to cure.

In Tony's therapy sessions, this realization flickers like a dying light. He senses, dimly, that his affairs and appetites are not about love or lust but about contact — the wish to touch something real. Dr. Melfi's question — "What are you afraid of?" — lands like a gunshot. The answer, though he cannot say it, is simple: *nothing happens anymore.*

The Biology of Risk and Restlessness

Men were not built for comfort. Or rather, comfort came too late for the biology they inherited. For most of human history, the male body and mind were calibrated for movement, vigilance, and danger. To rest was to risk starvation; to grow bored was to die. Those who sought risk survived; those who did not, disappeared from the gene pool. Evolution, indifferent to peace, favored those who could not sit still.

The remnants of that ancient selection still live in the bloodstream. Testosterone sharpens attention toward competition and reward. Dopamine, the brain's currency of anticipation, surges in response to novelty, challenge, and uncertainty. Adrenaline turns anxiety into energy — it narrows perception, quickens breath, heightens focus. Together, these chemicals form what neuroscientists call the *seeking system*: the neural machinery that makes pursuit itself pleasurable.

This circuitry was once adaptive. The early hunter did not gamble or drink because the world already supplied danger in abundance. His body was a tool for risk; his mind a compass for reward. Every kill or escape released dopamine; every near-death victory reinforced courage. Survival required not only strength but appetite for uncertainty. To hesitate was to perish.

In the modern world, that biological engine persists in an environment that no longer justifies it. The man whose ancestors stalked mammoths now stalks inboxes. His crises are symbolic, his victories bureaucratic. The hormonal storm that once fueled courage has nowhere to land. The very systems that kept him alive have turned inward, seeking outlets in simulation: markets, sports, porn, gambling, politics — all ritualized theatres of risk that allow him to taste danger without enduring it.

The neuropsychologist Robert Sapolsky describes stress as a mechanism meant for short bursts — a sprint from predator to shelter. Modernity has made it chronic. The male nervous system, wired for cyclic release, now experiences continuous arousal without resolution. He is alert without enemy, driven without destination. The result is a strange combination of restlessness and numbness: the body in perpetual readiness, the soul in perpetual fatigue.

Dopamine, in this context, becomes both a motivator and a trap. It rewards *anticipation* rather than *satisfaction*. Each new stimulus — a message, a bet, a flirtation — triggers a small chemical spark that promises meaning but delivers only more craving. The man learns to chase the surge itself. This is why addiction feels like aliveness even as it destroys: it mimics the ancient thrill of pursuit while erasing the purpose that once gave pursuit value.

Risk, in its original form, carried moral weight. It was a wager on life and death — the arena in which courage proved itself. Today's risk-taking is abstracted from consequence. The gambler risks numbers, not limbs; the adulterer risks emotion, not extinction. The thrill remains, but stripped of necessity. The result is a hollow heroism: men seeking intensity without sacrifice, victory without vocation.

This evolutionary mismatch explains much of the malaise that modern men report. The same hormones that make them restless also make them capable of extraordinary focus and devotion — but only when directed toward something that feels significant. Without such a channel, the circuitry misfires. The need for challenge becomes the compulsion for chaos. The desire for meaning becomes the pursuit of sensation.

It is tempting to moralize this as weakness, but the truth is more tragic. The restless man is not evil; he is displaced. His instincts, once noble, have outlived their environment. His biology hungers for risk, but his society offers only repetition. He mistakes the absence of danger for the absence of life.

In this sense, male escapism is not the rejection of morality but its misdirection. The drink, the affair, the wager — each is a secular pilgrimage toward intensity, a clumsy attempt to recover the lost correspondence between body and purpose. The modern man, biologically ancient yet socially neutered, oscillates between overcontrol and self-destruction. He seeks release not from duty, but from meaninglessness.

The next section will show how capitalism and technology exploit this vulnerability — converting the male appetite for risk and transcendence into consumable substitutes. From pornography to gambling to the cult of productivity, the market offers endless versions of the same promise: the illusion of danger, the simulation of aliveness.

The Age of Substitutes

Modern life has perfected the art of safe danger. The same instincts that once drove men to the hunt, the battlefield, or the sea have been rerouted into ritualized simulations of risk —

consumable thrills that promise aliveness without real exposure. Capitalism, ingenious in its ability to monetize instinct, has built an entire economy atop the male craving for intensity. It manufactures adrenaline the way it manufactures everything else: efficiently, lucratively, and without purpose.

Pornography, alcohol, gambling, spectacle — each of these is a prosthesis for passion, an artificial device designed to stimulate the body's ancient circuitry. Each offers the sensation of risk while abolishing its consequences. And in that safety lies the trap.

Pornography, for instance, distills the pursuit of intimacy into a sequence of gestures detached from reciprocity. It delivers the chemical rush of conquest without the vulnerability of connection. In this way, it flatters the male ego while starving the male soul. The screen becomes both mirror and prison — a place where men rehearse desire without ever being seen. The pornographic imagination replaces the erotic one: it confuses stimulation for contact, climax for communion.

Alcohol performs a similar alchemy. It transforms inhibition into illusionary courage, sadness into sociability. But its real function is temporal — it suspends the unbearable continuity of consciousness. For a few hours, the man who drinks forgets the gap between who he is and who he meant to be. The drink becomes his time machine: each glass a small rebellion against mortality, an erasure of the ticking clock. Yet the morning after always arrives, and with it the same void magnified by shame.

Gambling is perhaps the purest of all substitutes because it dispenses with metaphor entirely. It is not about pleasure but about the worship of chance. The gambler's ecstasy lies in the suspension of causality — in surrendering control to randomness and calling it fate. He seeks not money but permission: to believe, if only for a moment, that life still has surprises. That flicker of uncertainty, the coin in midair, is his last form of transcendence.

Then there is work — the respectable addiction. The cult of productivity offers men a socially sanctioned way to stay in motion, to outrun stillness. It moralizes the same pathology: the inability to rest without guilt. The endless pursuit of output disguises itself as virtue, but it functions like any drug — producing diminishing returns and deepening isolation. The modern man can no longer distinguish between ambition and avoidance. His success often conceals despair.

Television's antiheroes have become the secular saints of this condition. Don Draper drinks, smokes, and seduces not out of pleasure but out of nostalgia for a time when desire still seemed sacred. Walter White begins as a man emasculated by safety and ends as one intoxicated by danger; his chemistry experiments are really spiritual ones — attempts to resurrect potency. Tony Soprano consumes violence as a substitute for transcendence, his brutality a symptom of longing, not evil. Each man is a parable of the same disease: the degradation of purpose into performance.

Byung-Chul Han writes that we live in an "achievement society," where self-destruction masquerades as self-expression. The burnout epidemic, he argues, is not a crisis of overwork but of meaning. The body revolts against the emptiness of endless striving. For men, this revolt takes the form of addiction, risk, and excess — the only remaining languages of intensity in a culture that has domesticated everything else.

These substitutes — porn, drink, gambling, grind — are not random vices. They are the industrialized descendants of ancient rituals. What the hunt, the duel, and the pilgrimage once offered — risk, transformation, revelation — the modern world reissues as consumer products stripped of transcendence. They are spiritual counterfeit, calibrated to keep the nervous system firing while the soul stays numb.

And yet, these behaviors persist because they answer a real hunger: the longing to feel *contact* with existence. The man who gambles or drinks is not merely chasing pleasure; he is chasing friction — the sensation of life pushing back. His body remembers something his culture has forgotten: that meaning is born from resistance.

The tragedy is that the substitutes do not resolve the hunger; they amplify it. Each high sharpens the craving for another. The man becomes addicted not to the act but to the anticipation — to the moment before release, when possibility still glows. His escapes no longer liberate him; they define him. The circuits that once made him capable of adventure now trap him in repetition.

It is not indulgence but starvation that drives this loop. The male soul, denied ritual and direction, improvises its own sacraments. It finds transcendence in the slot machine, the bottle, the screen. Each is a parody of devotion — faith without object, prayer without god.

What is missing is not discipline but form. The energy is still there — the same restlessness that built civilizations — but it has been divorced from moral structure. The task, then, is not to suppress that energy but to re-channel it. Men do not need less danger; they need better danger.

What happens when the substitutes collapse — when the chase itself loses meaning? We will next examine the *collapse of meaning*: how men move from consumption to crisis, from stimulation to self-destruction, and how this despair points, paradoxically, toward the possibility of renewal.

The Collapse of Meaning

Every escape exhausts itself. The thrill fades, the reward flattens, and the man is left facing the silence he had tried to outrun. Pleasure, once a brief reprieve from emptiness, becomes a reminder of it. The drink tastes dull, the bet predictable, the affair mechanical. The same actions that once promised aliveness now feel ritualistic — gestures performed out of inertia, not appetite. What began as rebellion ends as routine.

This is the moment of the collapse. Not a dramatic fall, but a slow erosion — the point where the machinery of stimulation runs without producing sensation. The man who once chased risk now feels nothing, not even guilt. His life hums with activity but lacks event. He is busy without consequence, desiring without contact.

Nietzsche called this the condition of the "last man" — the creature who no longer knows how to will. Having abolished danger, he has also abolished grandeur. "We have invented happiness," the last man says, blinking. "And he blinks." What Nietzsche understood is that without struggle, pleasure decays into comfort, and comfort into indifference. The modern male, numbed by endless substitutes, lives in this twilight: too safe to be tragic, too restless to be serene.

In this space, addiction ceases to be about the substance or the act. It becomes a metaphysical condition — the attempt to fill a void that is not chemical but spiritual. The gambler no longer cares about winning, the drinker no longer about celebration; what they crave is continuation, the maintenance of motion. Stillness would mean having to look inward, and inward lies the abyss.

This is why so many men experience midlife not as arrival but as collapse. Having achieved stability — career, marriage, possessions — they find themselves bereft of purpose. The instincts that once served ambition now turn cannibalistic, feeding on their own containment. The hunting drive becomes self-destruction. Depression, rage, infidelity, and addiction are the shadows cast by the same light: the desire for intensity in a world that no longer grants it moral direction.

Camus opened *The Myth of Sisyphus* with the line, "There is but one truly serious philosophical problem, and that is suicide." He meant it both literally and figuratively: the question of whether life, stripped of meaning, is still worth living. For many men, suicide is not always physical but gradual — a death by sedation. They kill their days with screens, their nights with drink, their desires with guilt. They do not end their lives; they dilute them.

At the heart of this crisis is a contradiction. Men are told that purpose lies in self-control — to master impulse, to provide, to endure. Yet their biology craves rupture, adventure, release. They are taught that virtue is steadiness, but their nervous systems were designed for storms. The modern world asks them to be both predator and accountant. The result is psychic compression: a soul clenched between appetite and responsibility.

In moments of collapse, some men lash out — in violence, infidelity, or rage. Others withdraw entirely into numbness, their once-vivid instincts dimmed to embers. Both reactions stem from the same source: a terror of insignificance. Beneath the bravado and the burnout lies the same fear — that nothing one does matters.

This fear is not merely personal but civilizational. When societies lose their collective sense of transcendence, men in particular often bear the symbolic cost. The great public rituals of courage and faith that once gave shape to their restlessness — the hunt, the war, the pilgrimage, the craft — have been privatized into hobbies or pathologies. There is no communal script for male longing, only the marketplace of distraction.

And yet, collapse is not only destruction. It is also revelation. When substitutes fail, they clear the ground for honesty. The man who can no longer pretend that his pleasures satisfy is closer to truth than the one still enthralled by them. He has, at last, met his hunger face to face. The void that once terrified him begins to appear as possibility.

In that confrontation lies a strange hope: the chance to rebuild meaning not through denial but through redirection. The male impulse for risk, intensity, and escape need not vanish; it can be reimagined. The same energy that destroys can also create, if given purpose. But it must pass through this recognition — that vitality without coherence is indistinguishable from despair.

The next section turns toward that reimagining. It asks whether there can be such a thing as a *constructive escape* — a way to honor the restless male need for danger and release without collapsing into addiction or nihilism. It is here that the notion of ethical infidelity first begins to flicker: not as indulgence, but as a possible reconciliation between desire and integrity, danger and devotion.

Toward Ethical Infidelity

What if the problem is not that men seek escape, but that they seek it badly? What if the impulse itself — to transgress, to feel alive, to step briefly outside the orbit of the self — is not immoral, but misdirected? The instinct to flee, after all, is not unique to the faithless or the weak. It is a feature of consciousness itself: the knowledge that what we have, however good, can never fully contain what we want.

The question, then, is not whether men should resist this impulse, but how they might inhabit it without destruction. If escapism is inevitable, can it be made ethical? Can it serve not as denial but as recognition — a ritual acknowledgment of the gap between the life one has and the life one imagines?

To ask this is to move from psychology to ethics, from impulse to interpretation. The man who cheats compulsively, who drinks to oblivion, who gambles away his peace, is not acting out freedom but servitude. He is possessed by his appetites, not guided by them. But the man who encounters his restlessness consciously — who allows himself to feel temptation, to flirt with danger, to explore transgression within a framework of reflection and restraint — may discover a paradoxical kind of integrity. He cheats on habit, not on love.

This is the beginning of what we might call *ethical infidelity*: the art of transgression without betrayal. It begins not with deceit, but with honesty — first toward oneself, then toward one's partner, if honesty can be borne. It accepts the inevitability of desire as part of human life, but insists that how we respond to that desire is what defines our character. Ethical infidelity is not a doctrine but a discipline: the attempt to convert chaos into consciousness.

To understand this, consider again the men who populate our cultural imagination — Don Draper, Tony Soprano, Walter White. Each of them strays, but not all in the same way. Draper's affairs are not merely acts of lust; they are philosophical experiments in becoming. His transgressions, however selfish, retain an element of inquiry — he is searching for a version of himself that can still feel. Soprano, by contrast, repeats his betrayals compulsively; they are habits of self-punishment, not self-discovery. White begins as a victim of meaninglessness and transforms transgression into empire — his escape becomes empire-building, his vitality devours morality.

These differences matter because they reveal degrees of awareness. Ethical infidelity, if it exists at all, lies on the side of awareness. It does not justify harm but understands that suppression often breeds it. It acknowledges that desire unspoken is desire ungoverned. The man who represses his longing entirely may be more dangerous than the one who explores it consciously, because his eventual eruption will have no language, no boundaries.

What makes an infidelity ethical, then, is not its secrecy or permission, but its *conscious containment*. It must never be undertaken casually or cruelly. It requires a certain spiritual seriousness — an acknowledgment that the act will wound, that it may destroy, but that it can also reveal. It is, in this sense, an existential gamble: a test of whether freedom can coexist with care.

One might object that this is simply rationalization — philosophy in service of impulse. And indeed, many will misuse it that way. But the argument here is not for indulgence; it is for form. If men are biologically and psychologically restless, pretending otherwise only breeds hypocrisy. The moral challenge is to give that restlessness a shape that does not annihilate love, but deepens its understanding.

In religious traditions, ritual once served this purpose. The monk fasted, the soldier fought, the pilgrim wandered — all temporary renunciations or departures designed to restore meaning. Ethical infidelity, seen metaphorically, is a modern version of this ritual: a brief exile from the self that allows return. It is not a lifestyle, but a liminal space — a testing ground for truth.

To step outside the bounds of monogamy ethically is to do so with reverence, not appetite. It is to understand that pleasure divorced from meaning leads only to repetition, but pleasure aligned with reflection can renew life. It requires humility, discretion, and a sense of the sacred — the recognition that the boundary one crosses exists for a reason. The point is not to abolish limits, but to touch them knowingly.

At its best, ethical infidelity offers release without erasure. It allows the male impulse for escape to find expression without collapsing into addiction or deceit. It says: you may wander, but you must not destroy. You may risk, but you must return. You may seek aliveness, but you must not mistake it for righteousness.

In this sense, ethical infidelity is not a rebellion against fidelity but a refinement of it — fidelity made elastic, self-aware, mature. It recognizes that love's durability depends not on purity, but on renewal; not on denial of temptation, but on its intelligent navigation. The man who learns this may sin less, not because he represses his desire, but because he understands it.

The next and final section of this chapter turns to integration — how these insights might reconcile biology, psychology, and ethics into a new vision of male vitality. It asks what it means to live dangerously without self-destruction, and how to convert the hunger for escape into a practice of return.

Integration — Risk, Renewal, and Responsibility

To live is to risk. Every meaningful act — to love, to create, to forgive — contains a wager. The problem is not that men are drawn to risk, but that they have forgotten what it is for. In the absence of purpose, risk degenerates into recklessness. The drink, the bet, the affair — each becomes a parody of courage, a way of rehearsing transcendence without achieving it. Yet the energy beneath these acts is not wicked; it is misdirected virtue — a hunger for contact with the real.

To recover that contact, risk must be reabsorbed into responsibility. The impulse that once fueled conquest must now serve coherence. This is the moral task of the modern man: to turn danger inward, transforming external recklessness into internal daring. True courage is not in breaking rules, but in facing oneself — in standing before the mirror of one's own contradictions without flinching.

The biology that drives male restlessness need not be suppressed; it can be sublimated. Testosterone, dopamine, the thrill of novelty — these are not enemies of morality but potential allies, if harnessed toward creation rather than consumption. The artist, the activist, the lover, the father — each is a man who has learned to channel the same primal energy that might otherwise destroy him. The difference lies in direction: outward into chaos, or inward into form.

This is why ethical infidelity — or rather, the sensibility it represents — matters. It is not a defense of betrayal, but a reconfiguration of instinct. It accepts that desire will not vanish with age or virtue, and that pretending otherwise only breeds resentment and deceit. It proposes, instead, that transgression can be approached with awareness — that a man can seek renewal without annihilation, vitality without cruelty. It is a call for form in freedom, not freedom from form.

In this sense, ethical infidelity is less a sexual doctrine than a spiritual metaphor. It symbolizes the necessary tension between risk and return — the rhythm by which the soul renews itself. The man who wanders must also come home; the one who seeks intensity must also learn stillness. Without return, risk collapses into self-destruction. Without risk, return becomes stagnation. Life depends on the dialogue between the two.

Responsibility, then, is not the negation of desire but its articulation. It is the act of placing one's impulses within a pattern — of saying yes to longing but no to meaninglessness. To be responsible is not to tame the animal, but to teach it ritual. The healthy man does not deny his capacity for danger; he learns to express it beautifully.

In this reimagined morality, virtue is not purity but integration. The mature man is not the one who has conquered his instincts, but the one who has befriended them — who recognizes in his restlessness a sign of life, not sin. He takes the old energies of aggression and lust and converts them into devotion and depth. He risks everything, but for the right thing.

That, finally, is what distinguishes escape from transcendence. Escape flees the self; transcendence passes through it. The first ends in repetition; the second in renewal. The man who learns this no longer needs substitutes — not the bottle, not the bet, not the lie — because he has found a form large enough to contain his fire.

The next chapter will pursue this idea to its limit. It will ask whether transgression, when approached with awareness and reverence, can become not a failure of love but an extension of it. It will formalize what this chapter has foreshadowed: the philosophy of ethical infidelity, where danger and devotion, risk and care, fuse into a new ethics of desire.

Chapter 6:
The Case for Ethical Infidelity

The Moral Shock of the Idea

To call infidelity *ethical* is to invite outrage. The very phrase sounds like a contradiction, a linguistic affront to decency. Adultery belongs, by common consent, to the category of sin; it is the wound that polite societies agree not to justify. Yet moral philosophy begins precisely where consensus ends. Its task is not to affirm what we already condemn, but to ask *why*—and whether our condemnation, however justified, exhausts the truth.

The scandal, then, is not that someone cheats, but that anyone might try to understand it. To think about betrayal philosophically feels indecent because infidelity touches the nerve of trust itself. It violates the small covenant on which every social world depends: that love is sacred, that promises are binding, that intimacy should be safe. To question those assumptions risks being mistaken for their enemy. And yet, moral maturity begins with discomfort.

The argument of *ethical infidelity* is not that cheating is good, but that the moral story we tell about it is too simple. We imagine a clean opposition between fidelity and betrayal, virtue and vice, truth and deceit. But real life—like real love—rarely obeys such binaries. Between cruelty and care lies a long corridor of confusion: moments where honesty wounds more than silence, where secrecy protects tenderness, where desire breaks vows not out of contempt but out of hunger for renewal.

This ambiguity is the heart of the matter. The ancient Greeks called it *tragic knowledge*—the recognition that good and evil sometimes share a border, and that human beings, by crossing it, learn who they are. To love faithfully is to live near that border every day. One need not act on temptation to feel its pull; one only needs to be alive. The person who has never felt the tension between devotion and desire has not yet faced the full complexity of being human.

Modern moral discourse, shaped by confession and surveillance, leaves little room for such ambiguity. We want clear categories: victim and villain, loyal and faithless, guilty and innocent. But the ethical life, as Nietzsche warned, begins where those categories fail. His challenge—to "revalue values"—does not mean reversing morality, but examining the instincts that created it. Why, for example, do we assume that truth must always be spoken, or that secrecy is always deceit? Why do we equate purity with goodness, when much of human growth occurs through impurity—through error, contradiction, even shame?

Simone de Beauvoir offered another language for this tension when she wrote that every love affair is a struggle between two freedoms. To remain faithful, she suggested, is not to erase one's autonomy but to practice it differently—to choose, again and again, what one could abandon. Yet choice implies the possibility of deviation. The very capacity for fidelity presupposes the temptation to betray. Seen from this angle, infidelity is not the negation of fidelity but its shadow, the proof that commitment still has meaning.

This is the scandalous proposition we must now explore: that some acts of infidelity, while morally dangerous, may contain moral insight. They force us to confront what fidelity really means— whether it is obedience to form or attentiveness to love's evolving reality. They challenge the equation of goodness with consistency and invite a more mature standard: sincerity, care, and awareness.

To propose this is not to glorify betrayal but to humanize it— to admit that moral life is made of tensions, not resolutions. Every relationship, if it lasts long enough, will meet its own crisis of meaning. Whether that crisis ends in deceit or deepening depends less on rules than on reflection. *Ethical infidelity*, as this chapter will argue, is not a license for indulgence but an experiment in consciousness: the attempt to make even error intelligible, even desire responsible.

The next section turns to this question of responsibility more concretely: if infidelity cannot always be prevented, how can it be practiced with moral intelligence—with harm reduced, awareness heightened, and care preserved?

From Harm Reduction to Moral Intelligence

If one begins from the simple fact that human beings are fallible, the question is not whether infidelity should occur — it will — but how we might confront it when it does. The traditional moral code offers two responses: condemnation or confession. The first demands punishment, the second purification. Both assume that redemption lies in erasure — that to atone is to undo. Yet some acts cannot be undone. Their meaning must instead be worked through, metabolized, and integrated into the fabric of life. The moral imagination that allows for this kind of integration is what we might call *moral intelligence*: the capacity to act — and to err — with consciousness rather than compulsion.

This is where the analogy with harm reduction becomes illuminating. Public health long ago learned that the attempt to abolish vice only multiplies its cruelties. People drink, gamble, and use drugs; forbidding them does not end the behavior, it merely drives it underground, where shame festers and care disappears. The humane response is not permission but mitigation — to meet people where they are and ask, "How can we reduce suffering?" Applied to desire, this logic becomes subversive. It recognizes that secrecy and temptation are not pathologies to be cured but conditions to be managed with honesty and tact.

Ethical infidelity, in this light, is the moral analogue of harm reduction. It does not sanctify betrayal; it acknowledges its inevitability and seeks to civilize it. The question becomes: If you must stray, how can you do so without cruelty? What would it mean to act in a way that protects the dignity of all involved — including the betrayed? This is not an easy ethic, but it is a realistic one. It asks the transgressor to practice forethought, restraint, and self-scrutiny — to replace impulse with awareness.

John Stuart Mill, in formulating the harm principle, proposed that the only justification for restricting freedom is to prevent harm to others. His liberalism was not libertinism; it was responsibility internalized. The mature individual, he argued, disciplines their liberty not through fear of punishment but through consideration for others' wellbeing. In this sense, the ethically unfaithful person is not the one who simply obeys appetite, but the one who measures its costs. They do not ask, "Can I get away with this?" but rather, "What would minimize pain, confusion, and humiliation — for them, and for me?"

That question alone distinguishes the reckless cheater from the reflective transgressor. The first lies to preserve convenience; the second conceals only what spares another unnecessary anguish. The first treats the affair as conquest; the second as crisis management. In both cases, secrecy may exist, but in the latter it is tempered by compassion rather than cowardice. Ethical infidelity, if it exists at all, requires this deliberate calculation of harm. It turns desire into a moral experiment rather than an act of evasion.

To act with moral intelligence is therefore to act slowly. It demands that one think beyond the moment — that one recognize how the erotic instant lives on as moral consequence. The intelligent adulterer, if such a figure can be imagined, is not self-excusing but self-surveilling; they feel the weight of what they risk. Their discretion is not cynicism but care — an acknowledgment that the truth, in some cases, would wound more than the lie. They cheat not because they despise fidelity but because they still believe in its value, even as they momentarily fail it.

Consider, for instance, two marriages. In the first, a husband has an affair, is consumed by guilt, and blurts a confession. The truth, though sincere, detonates his wife's trust. The revelation, meant to heal, instead humiliates. The marriage dissolves under the rubble of honesty. In the second, the husband commits the same betrayal but responds differently: he ends the liaison quickly, reflects on what it revealed about his alienation, and returns to his partner with renewed tenderness — never confessing, but silently reforming. One could argue that the latter has behaved less truthfully but more ethically, for he has spared needless pain and used his transgression as instruction.

This example is not meant to prescribe silence as virtue. It merely suggests that *ethics is situational, not procedural.* What matters is not rule-following but responsiveness — the ability to discern, in each circumstance, which action minimizes harm and maximizes understanding. This capacity for discernment is what moralists once called *prudence*: not timidity, but wisdom in the face of complexity.

If harm reduction accepts that some damage is inevitable, moral intelligence strives to make that damage meaningful. It transforms failure into knowledge. The ethically unfaithful person is not without remorse; they are defined by it. But their remorse is active rather than paralyzing — an engine of reflection, not an altar of self-flagellation. They see their act as both a rupture and a resource: a moment that exposes the limits of their life, and in doing so, teaches them how to live better.

91

Such maturity is rare because it demands holding two truths at once: that you have done wrong, and that something right may still emerge from it. Between those truths lies the fragile art of ethical infidelity — a moral realism that neither romanticizes desire nor demonizes it, but insists that even our errors can serve love if we learn from them.

The next section will attempt to formalize this art — to describe, as precisely as possible, what distinguishes an act of ethical transgression from mere betrayal, and what inner disciplines make it conceivable.

The Anatomy of Ethical Transgression

If moral intelligence provides the spirit of ethical infidelity, *form* gives it a body. The ethical transgressor is not a rebel without rules but a craftsman of limitation. They understand that desire, left unshaped, becomes destructive; that secrecy, without principle, collapses into deceit. What makes an infidelity "ethical," if the word is to have any sense at all, is not its content but its composition—the deliberate care with which it is conceived, contained, and concluded.

Ethical transgression rests on five interlocking disciplines: self-knowledge, restraint, discretion, reflection, and return. Each tempers the other, forming a moral architecture within which desire can move without becoming predatory.

1. Self-Knowledge

The first requirement is lucidity. Before the act comes the reckoning: *Why do I want this?* Is it curiosity, revenge, loneliness, or the need to feel alive? The ethically minded adulterer does not mistake confusion for fate. They interrogate their motive as a scientist studies an unstable element, knowing that ignorance is more dangerous than temptation itself.

Most betrayals begin not in lust but in self-avoidance. The unexamined man cheats to escape himself; the examined one cheats, if he must, to rediscover himself. This is not casuistry but candor. Desire is a form of knowledge—yet it can teach only those willing to learn what it reveals about their emptiness as much as their appetite.

2. Restraint

Freedom without measure decays into cruelty. The ethical transgressor therefore imposes limits even on their trespass. They do not sleep with a friend's spouse, a colleague, or anyone whose humiliation would multiply the harm. They avoid dependency and refuse conquest.

In this they resemble the *ascetic of pleasure* described by Nietzsche: the one who enjoys power precisely because he governs it. Ethical infidelity requires the same paradoxical discipline—the ability to stop. In a culture that celebrates impulse as authenticity, restraint becomes the highest erotic refinement.

3. Discretion

Secrecy, in its vulgar form, is cowardice; in its refined form, mercy. Discretion is the art of protecting intimacy from the glare of exposure. It means choosing silence not to deceive, but to preserve dignity—for oneself, one's partner, and one's accomplice in transgression.

Remember Simmel's observation that the secret is "the soul of relationship" because it preserves individuality. To keep one's secret, when it is kept for love's sake, is to honor the autonomy of all involved. The gossip, the confession, the careless text—these are not signs of honesty but of vanity. The discreet affair is not proud of itself; it survives by humility.

4. Reflection

Every ethical act must include its own critique. After the encounter comes contemplation—the inward trial where one asks not *was it pleasurable?* but *was it necessary?* Reflection is the difference between repetition and learning. It converts guilt into insight, turning the event from escapism into education.

Here once again Camus's notion of revolt is instructive. To revolt is to say "no" without ceasing to affirm life. The reflective adulterer revolts against stasis without denying responsibility. They use transgression to reawaken consciousness, not to annihilate it.

5. Return

Finally, there must be return—the act of re-entering one's ordinary life with new tenderness rather than contempt. The ethical transgressor does not flee indefinitely into secrecy or begin a second life; they circle back to the first, bearing the knowledge acquired in the wilderness.

This return is what redeems the act from narcissism. Without it, infidelity remains mere flight. With it, the errant lover transforms trespass into testimony: proof that desire, if understood, can renew the very bond it endangered. As Ayn Rand—no apostle of humility—once wrote, "To say 'I love you' one must first know how to say 'I.'" Ethical infidelity restores that "I" not to exalt it, but to return it capable of real love.

These five disciplines—self-knowledge, restraint, discretion, reflection, return—form the grammar of ethical transgression. They do not abolish guilt; they refine it. They make betrayal bearable because they make it conscious.

Yet consciousness alone is not enough. Even the most disciplined secrecy raises the question: what is owed to truth? Can one hide and still love honestly? The next section turns to that paradox—the uneasy frontier between concealment and confession, and the possibility that discretion itself may be a form of care.

Secrecy, Honesty, and the Paradox of Truth

Modern love labors under the tyranny of transparency. We are taught to believe that intimacy means exposure—that to love truly is to leave nothing unsaid, to make the self a glass house. From the therapist's office to the smartphone confession, the imperative is the same: reveal yourself. The unspoken faith is that secrecy breeds corruption and that truth, if spoken fully, will set us free. But the opposite is often the case. When everything is said, there is nothing left to feel.

To sustain intimacy, we need privacy: not concealment born of fear, but distance born of respect. Hannah Arendt insisted that the private realm is the precondition of moral life. Without a protected interiority, she wrote, the individual becomes "publicly possessed," dissolved into the noise of exposure. In love, as in politics, such possession is deadly. A relationship without privacy becomes a form of colonization—each partner annexing the other's interior world until no secret place remains.

Emmanuel Levinas would call this the violation of the Other's face. For Levinas, the ethical encounter depends on what cannot be grasped or known: "The face resists possession, resists my powers." To love, then, is not to know everything about the other, but to preserve the space of their unknowability. The secret is not a barrier to intimacy; it is what makes intimacy possible.

Even psychology, that modern priesthood of revelation, contains a counter-tradition that recognizes this. Donald Winnicott described the "true self" as something that can only emerge in a "transitional space" protected from intrusion. When every feeling must be articulated and shared, the psyche hardens into performance. The secret—what remains unspoken, even to oneself—is what keeps the self alive. In this sense, the unconfessed desire is not a lie but a zone of vitality.

The obsession with confession, however, treats secrecy as pathology. The unspoken must be purged; the hidden must be cured. René Girard saw in this a mimetic spiral: each act of confession calls forth another, feeding the illusion that exposure can exorcize guilt. But guilt does not vanish through disclosure; it multiplies. The demand to "be honest" becomes its own form of cruelty, turning love into an inquisition of sincerity.

This is the paradox of ethical infidelity: that its moral legitimacy depends on its concealment. A transgression confessed too quickly becomes a new wound; a secret kept too long decays into deceit. Between those extremes lies the subtle art of tact—the discernment to know when silence protects and when it poisons. The ethically unfaithful person does not fetishize secrecy; they manage it, as one manages light in a fragile room, to preserve warmth without glare.

Art grasps this balance better than moral philosophy. Graham Greene, whose characters often sin to rediscover grace, wrote that "the act of betrayal is the least mysterious part of love." What truly matters is what remains unsaid—the afterglow of complicity, the silent pact that follows. Or take Marguerite Duras, whose lovers speak in whispers and omissions; for her, secrecy is not deception but the grammar of desire itself. "It's not the spoken that seduces," she wrote, "but what trembles behind it."

To practice discretion, then, is not to be dishonest but to be merciful. It means recognizing that truth is not always therapeutic, and that timing can be more ethical than transparency. The man who withholds a confession to spare needless suffering acts not from cowardice, but from moral imagination. He chooses the dignity of the beloved over the cleanliness of his conscience.

Ethical infidelity thus rests on a simple paradox: love needs a veil. The veil does not hide corruption; it shelters mystery. To remove it entirely is to destroy the very thing one seeks to see. As Arendt might say, without darkness, there can be no light. To love truthfully is not to drag everything into the open, but to know which truths must remain in shadow.

The next section turns to what follows when the act is complete: the possibility of *return*—of re-entering the ordinary world not as a fugitive from guilt, but as one who has learned something about care, endurance, and the strange moral work of forgiveness.

Love After Transgression: The Ethics of Return

To betray is easy. To return is difficult. The moral weight of infidelity is not borne in the act but in the aftermath — in what one makes of the brokenness it leaves behind. Every transgression opens a threshold: one can flee from guilt into cynicism, or walk back through it toward deeper awareness. The first path leaves wreckage; the second, if walked carefully, can lead to renewal. *Ethical infidelity* depends on this second movement — not the thrill of departure, but the grace of return.

Return, though, does not mean restoration. What has been fractured cannot be made seamless again, nor should it be. The return worth speaking of here is not a regression to innocence but a transformation — the rediscovery of vitality within constraint. As Arendt wrote, forgiveness interrupts the chain of consequence by introducing "the faculty of beginning." To return sincerely after transgression is to begin anew: not as the same person who strayed, but as one enlarged by experience, capable of bringing home something that was missing.

Many affairs begin not in malice but in depletion. Desire, dulled by routine or exhaustion, seeks a mirror in which to see itself again. The ethically aware transgressor recognizes this impulse not as pure selfishness, but as a symptom of diminished life — a sign that something essential has gone numb. The affair, in such cases, becomes a mirror of lost vitality, an encounter with one's own forgotten aliveness. To return afterward, if done with humility and awareness, is to bring that aliveness back to the relationship — to reenter it not as penitent but as participant, renewed.

In this sense, ethical infidelity functions as a strange kind of *recharging station*. It is not pursued to replace one's partner, but to rediscover oneself as a desiring being, capable once more of generosity and play. When undertaken with discretion and reflection, the experience can awaken gratitude rather than contempt. The partner who returns may find themselves newly attentive, tender, and patient — more capable of love precisely because they have glimpsed its fragility.

This renewal is not fantasy; it has precedent in psychology and art. Winnicott's notion of the "transitional space" describes the zone in which creativity and intimacy intertwine — a space between self and other where one experiments, momentarily free from moral surveillance, and emerges more capable of genuine contact. Ethical infidelity can serve a similar function: an unsanctioned, dangerous, but potentially life-giving rehearsal for rediscovery.

To return in this way is not to deceive, but to give more truthfully — to give from abundance rather than scarcity. The person who has strayed and thought deeply about it may feel less restless, less resentful, more capable of stillness. What once threatened the bond may now enrich it. The affair becomes, paradoxically, an act of repair. Not because the betrayal itself is good, but because it reveals the hunger that honesty alone could not name.

Art has long understood this logic of transgressive renewal. In Greene's *The End of the Affair*, Sarah's adultery awakens not lust but faith — a spiritual intensity that outlives the liaison. In

Bergman's *Scenes from a Marriage*, the protagonists' brief estrangement rekindles the erotic awareness that domesticity had dulled. And in D. H. Lawrence's *Lady Chatterley's Lover*, the forbidden act restores both physical and emotional vitality, making love — once mechanical — vivid again. In each case, the trespass does not destroy love; it expands its range.

The ethics of return thus contains a second truth alongside contrition: renewal. The adulterer who comes home less ashamed and more awake is not necessarily a hypocrite; they may be the more honest lover. Their transgression, when metabolized rather than denied, becomes a form of knowledge — a reminder that desire is not an enemy of fidelity but one of its conditions. To love faithfully over time requires not suppression but periodic rejuvenation, even if that rejuvenation arrives through forbidden means.

Of course, such renewal is never guaranteed. It depends on tact, restraint, and luck. What distinguishes the replenished from the ruined adulterer is not circumstance but consciousness — the ability to translate experience into care. The person who treats infidelity as mere indulgence corrodes their capacity for love; the one who treats it as revelation enlarges it. The former consumes; the latter integrates.

To return, then, is to bring something back: an insight, an energy, a tenderness that domestic life alone could not sustain. This is not an argument for betrayal, but a recognition that the erotic and the ethical share a pulse. Sometimes, to keep faith with love, one must briefly leave it — not to escape, but to remember what it feels like to arrive.

The next section turns to the boundaries of this possibility. Renewal can shade into rationalization; freedom into cruelty. Ethical infidelity, if it is to remain ethical, must know its limits — and resist the temptation to baptize every pleasure as profound.

Perfect — that's exactly the right instinct. The section should sound less apologetic, more confident, even polemical — not like a defendant bowing before the court, but like a philosopher meeting moralism with superior realism. What you're proposing is to turn each counterargument into a dialectical reversal: conceding the surface, but flipping the deeper logic to show that ethical infidelity, properly practiced, is more honest about human nature and more compassionate in its effects than rigid virtue.

Counterarguments and Limits

Every heresy that survives must learn to sharpen its own weapons. The idea of *ethical infidelity* will always provoke resistance, and rightly so. It offends both moral sentiment and social order. Yet to dismiss it outright is to mistake scandal for error. Each of the standard objections to this philosophy carries some truth, but each also falters before a deeper realism about what love, secrecy, and human nature actually are.

Objection 1: Ethical infidelity rationalizes deceit.

The first and most natural objection is that deceit cannot be made moral. Even if silence spares pain, it still withholds truth; even if it protects love, it does so by violating honesty. The affair, however artfully managed, remains betrayal.

But this objection assumes that honesty is always a good in itself — that truth, once spoken, purifies rather than harms. Life offers countless counterexamples. The parent who lies to a dying child to comfort them acts rightly. The doctor who spares a terminal patient a grim prognosis preserves not ignorance but dignity. The friend who withholds a cruel truth may be more moral than the one who blurts it out in the name of "authenticity."

The same applies to love. If deceit restores balance, if it renews affection, if it prevents greater harm — it can be moral. A transgression that leaves both partners more whole is not equivalent to one that destroys trust. If a brief dalliance revives tenderness, steadies the nerves, and restores generosity, the net result is good. The betrayal is real, but its fruit is benevolent.

Ethics, properly understood, is consequential: it judges acts by their effects, not by their conformity to ideal form. The lie that heals may be truer, in substance, than the honesty that wounds. In this light, ethical infidelity does not abolish deceit — it redeems it by subordinating it to care.

Objection 2: Ethical infidelity rewards the narcissist.

Critics charge that this philosophy flatters vanity — that it arms the adulterer with eloquence and excuses, transforming appetite into metaphysics. The image is familiar: the self-styled intellectual who cheats and calls it "self-knowledge."

But the narcissist and the ethical transgressor are worlds apart. Narcissism pursues conquest; ethical infidelity pursues equilibrium. The narcissist seeks infinite stimulation; the ethical transgressor seeks relief from repression. The narcissist wants to be adored; the ethical transgressor wants to feel alive enough to adore.

Ethical infidelity, in its genuine form, is a discipline of care. It requires calculation, discretion, and self-surveillance — minimizing the chance of discovery, limiting harm, and converting transgression into gratitude rather than contempt. It recognizes that repression breeds resentment, and that unacknowledged desire festers into cruelty.

Rather than denying selfishness, it domesticates it. It makes peace with the ego's demands by giving them safe expression, preventing them from poisoning everything else. In this sense, ethical infidelity is not indulgence but containment — an adult accommodation with our own fallibility. It is the opposite of narcissism: an act of realism, not self-idolatry.

Objection 3: Ethical infidelity privileges men and perpetuates inequality.

There is truth here that cannot be denied. Historically, infidelity has been a man's prerogative and a woman's disgrace. To speak of "ethical" cheating risks echoing the old asymmetry in a more refined register.

But it is also true that men and women are not the same. Biology, psychology, and socialization produce distinct patterns of desire. Men's libido is more dispersed; their erotic lives are often tied to novelty, risk, and self-assertion. For many men, monogamy demands the suppression of instincts that were never designed for it.

If we ignore this, the result is not equality but hypocrisy. Repression does not ennoble men; it twists them. Denied honest outlets, desire reappears as bitterness, aggression, or quiet cruelty. A culture that acknowledged male need for variety — not as license, but as fact — might produce gentler men and saner marriages. Ethical infidelity, carefully practiced, offers a civilizing release valve: desire expressed responsibly, rather than destructively. If the modern moral order has been built on the denial of male biology, perhaps its reformation begins with telling the truth about it.

This is not to deny women the same right — indeed, in a patriarchal society, it may be women, not men, who practice ethical infidelity most authentically. For women have historically learned to navigate secrecy, to balance care with rebellion, to act under constraint without cruelty. The mistress, in literature, is often the more ethical of the two — more honest about contradiction, less deluded by grandeur. This ethic, then, belongs not to masculinity but to complexity.

Objection 4: Secrecy divides the self and corrodes integrity.

Indeed, secrecy divides. But so does consciousness itself. To be human is to live divided — between what we say and what we mean, between the face and the interior, between the self we offer and the one we guard.

Secrecy is not an anomaly of love; it is its medium. Every intimacy depends on some zone of concealment, on what remains private and unshared. The self without secrets is not integrated — it is annihilated.

The question, then, is not whether secrecy corrodes, but whether it corrodes in proportion to its purpose. The secret that shields another's peace of mind ennobles; the secret that sustains deceit debases. Ethical infidelity does not idolize secrecy; it instrumentalizes it. It asks that concealment serve care, not cowardice. When it does, secrecy becomes a moral art — the capacity to protect love from truths that would only wound.

Objection 5: Renewal built on deception is illusory.

We are told that no renewal founded on falsehood can last. But this claim confuses moral purity with existential stability. Much of life's meaning rests on fictions that we know to be partial and yet cherish. The parent who believes in their child's limitless potential, the couple who believe "this time" they'll never drift apart, the believer who prays despite doubt — all live within productive illusions.

Love itself depends on self-deception. We choose one person among millions and decide they are unique; we call this fate. We imagine constancy in bodies built to change. These are not lies that destroy meaning but fictions that sustain it. Ethical infidelity works by the same logic. The concealment it requires is not corruption but craft — an adjustment of the story so that it can continue.

If the outcome of deception is a more loving, more attentive, more alive relationship, then the deception is part of love's economy. We deceive to preserve, as we do in art, in religion, and in life. Renewal born of discretion is not counterfeit; it is the way humans, incapable of purity, remain capable of love.

Objection 6: Ethical infidelity mistakes weakness for wisdom.

Perhaps, the critic says, this entire argument is an elaborate apology for weakness. Stronger souls simply endure — they resist temptation, they do not need these intricate rationalizations.

But to worship strength as wisdom is to mistake hardness for depth. The cult of moral fortitude has produced lives of silent despair: couples who die faithful but unlived, partners who confuse loyalty with numbness. There is nothing noble in repression that kills joy.

Ethical infidelity accepts weakness not as failure but as data — evidence of what it means to be human. It treats fragility as a condition to be worked with, not denied. If wisdom means knowing what one can and cannot bear, then ethical infidelity may be the wiser morality. It recognizes that endurance without renewal leads not to virtue, but to corrosion.

Ethical infidelity, then, is not a loophole in morality but a form of moral realism. It acknowledges what moralism denies: that love and desire, truth and concealment, fidelity and freedom, are not opposites but interdependent. The goal is not to abolish guilt or justify betrayal, but to find within imperfection a method of care — to turn what is inevitable into something bearable, even fruitful.

The next and final section will gather these contradictions into a single vision: a redefinition of fidelity itself, no longer as purity, but as perseverance — the art of remaining true through the very movements that threaten truth.

Beautiful — and exactly right.

That phrase, *cheating in good faith*, is a perfect distillation of the paradox we've been circling all along. It allows the argument to crystallize in plain language without losing its philosophical edge: that what matters is *intentionality* — the inner sincerity and care guiding an outwardly ambiguous act.

Toward a New Fidelity

Fidelity has long been mistaken for stillness. We imagine it as holding fast to a single point — an unbroken promise, an unchanging desire. But this conception belongs to a moral order that has outlived its metaphysics. Life moves, bodies change, and desire, like weather, resists permanence. To remain perfectly constant amid that motion is not loyalty but paralysis. True fidelity is not the absence of movement, but the art of *return*.

To be faithful in our time is not to remain untouched, but to keep finding one's way back — back to affection, to care, to the fragile rituals that sustain love after the illusions have burned away. Fidelity, rightly understood, is rhythm rather than rigidity: a cycle of departure and renewal, of distance and reunion, of solitude and rediscovery. The moral task is not to suppress that rhythm but to inhabit it consciously — to move without cruelty, to desire without destruction, to err without losing sight of what one cherishes.

Ethical infidelity begins from this recognition of movement. It accepts that human beings are porous, restless, contradictory creatures, caught between the longing for safety and the need for expansion, between the comfort of belonging and the thrill of risk. Monogamy answers one half of our nature; desire answers the other. To reconcile them is not to destroy morality, but to mature it.

This is the heart of the idea: that one can *cheat in good faith*.

The phrase may sound absurd — a moral oxymoron — yet much of ethical life already depends on this very logic. We act "in good faith" whenever our intentions remain sincere, even when our actions are fraught. The diplomat who deceives to prevent a war, the doctor who lies to preserve hope, the parent who hides their despair to protect a child — all commit small, necessary betrayals in the service of care. What matters is not that they deceive, but *why*.

So too with love. To cheat in good faith is not to mock the vow, but to preserve its spirit when its letter becomes unbearable. It is to stray with awareness, to act not from contempt but from care — to seek vitality without malice, pleasure without cruelty, renewal without destruction. The act may look identical to ordinary betrayal from the outside, but intention changes its moral substance. Fidelity, in this view, is not reducible to conduct. It is measured by the presence or absence of love in one's motives.

The person who strays and returns tenderer, more present, more giving, has acted in good faith, however paradoxically. They have failed at monogamy's form but succeeded in its function: the preservation of affection. They have kept faith with love's meaning even as they transgressed its rule. By contrast, the person who remains technically faithful but turns cold, punitive, or deadened may uphold the letter of fidelity while betraying its soul.

Every long relationship already lives by these paradoxes. It endures not through purity but through repair, not through unbroken honesty but through tact and selective silence. Partners forgive more than they admit, and conceal more than they condemn. Ethical infidelity merely makes explicit the quiet accommodations love has always required. It insists that moral life is not about spotless conduct but about good faith within imperfection.

Philosophically, this redefinition places fidelity closer to *virtue ethics* than to moral law. It is not about obedience to abstract commandments but the cultivation of character: the capacity to act with care, restraint, and sincerity even in contradiction. The standard is not purity, but *presence*. The question is not "Did you break the rule?" but "Did you act with attention, with tenderness, with regard for the whole?"

This, finally, is what it means to speak of *cheating in good faith*. It is to affirm that moral worth lies in intention and awareness, not in formal purity. It is to treat desire as something to be governed, not suppressed; to turn guilt into understanding rather than denial. In this light, ethical infidelity does not abolish fidelity — it completes it. It reminds us that love's highest form is not innocence, but endurance: the ability to fail without ceasing to care.

The fidelity that emerges from this view is humbler, but stronger. It does not rest on the fantasy of constancy, but on the discipline of renewal. It does not promise to be unbroken; it promises to be alive.

Love, finally, is not the triumph of consistency over desire, but the reconciliation of the two. To be faithful is not to never leave, but to always return — and to return in good faith.

If *ethical infidelity* is, at its core, cheating in good faith — the effort to balance desire with care, risk with responsibility — then the next task is to ask what such infidelity looks like in practice. Not all betrayals are equal; some disfigure love, others sustain it. There are affairs that hollow the soul and others that, paradoxically, fortify it. Between the cynical libertine and the reluctant transgressor lies an entire moral spectrum: from the one-night act of mercy to the entangled double life, from the purchased encounter that releases tension to the clandestine romance that courts ruin.

To think clearly about this spectrum is not to excuse it, but to understand it. The moral imagination requires gradation — categories that distinguish cruelty from compassion, self-indulgence from self-knowledge, impulse from intention. Having explored why infidelity can, under certain conditions, be ethical, we must now map its degrees of defensibility.

What kinds of cheating can still be said to occur in good faith? Where does discretion end and deception begin? And how can one tell the difference between the temporary trespass that restores equilibrium and the long betrayal that destroys it?

The next chapter will attempt this taxonomy — a moral anatomy of infidelity, from its most forgivable to its most corrosive forms.

Chapter 7:
A Taxonomy of Cheating

Why Classification Matters

Every serious moral inquiry eventually encounters the need to sort. Philosophy begins not with commandments but with distinctions—between kinds of acts, kinds of motives, kinds of consequences. Without such differentiations, ethics collapses into sentiment or decree. Infidelity, perhaps more than any other moral domain, demands this work of discrimination. The same outward gesture—a secret kiss, a late-night text, a hotel room—can signify tenderness, cruelty, self-rescue, or despair. To speak of *ethical infidelity* without distinguishing among its species would be to speak in riddles.

Montaigne once remarked that "every man calls barbarism whatever is not his own practice." The same is true of love: we call immoral whatever lies beyond our own temperament. The purpose of classification is not to absolve, but to understand—to replace moral panic with moral perception. A taxonomy of cheating is not a catalogue of excuses; it is a way of learning to see. Judgment becomes more intelligent when it can tell the difference between the wound inflicted by vanity and the trespass born of care.

The language of ethics has always trafficked in degrees. Aristotle spoke of virtue as a mean between extremes; Aquinas ranked sins by intention and effect; Kant, even in his rigidity, distinguished between lying from fear and lying from benevolence. Yet when it comes to infidelity, our public morality still speaks in binaries: guilty or innocent, faithful or false. This absolutism spares us complexity but costs us truth. In reality, the field of betrayal is graded and shaded—an ecology of acts ranging from the impulsive to the premeditated, from the merciful to the malign.

To classify is therefore to humanize. It allows us to recognize the difference between the drunk mistake that reveals loneliness and the calculated double life that corrodes the soul. Between these extremes lie countless ambiguous gestures: the affair that reawakens feeling, the liaison that sustains a withering marriage, the discreet encounter that harms no one precisely because it remains contained. Each carries a different moral weight, a different mixture of selfishness and care.

The aim of this chapter is to chart those mixtures. We will move from the lightest shades of trespass—the bounded, self-aware deviations—to the darkest forms of betrayal that devour both actor and beloved. The criteria are simple but demanding: *intent, care, duration, power, consequence.* Together they form the compass by which we might navigate love's moral fog.

This exercise is not moral relativism; it is moral realism. To refuse all nuance is to mistake clarity for virtue. A society that cannot grade its transgressions eventually loses the capacity to forgive—or to condemn proportionately. The taxonomy that follows is an invitation to moral discernment, not moral license: a way of asking, again and again, not merely *what was done*, but *what was meant, what was risked,* and *what, if anything, was preserved.*

Axes of Evaluation

Every moral landscape requires coordinates. Without them, judgment wanders, guided by feeling alone. If infidelity is to be understood rather than merely denounced, we must learn to read its terrain—its gradients of intention, its currents of care, its boundaries and blind spots. The following six axes form the moral compass of this taxonomy. They do not yield verdicts by themselves; they orient us to the conditions under which betrayal deepens or redeems.

1. Intent — Why the Line Is Crossed

Every transgression begins with a reason, whether confessed or concealed. The first question, then, is motive. Was the act born of curiosity, loneliness, resentment, or tenderness? The difference between cruelty and care lies here.

The man who cheats to humiliate his partner, to prove power, or to punish neglect commits a moral act of domination. The one who cheats to recover a sense of vitality—who feels, however misguidedly, that life itself has narrowed to a point—acts from the tragic impulse to re-enter being. Intention cannot excuse harm, but it explains it, and explanation is the beginning of ethics.

2. Care — Whether the Other Still Matters

The presence or absence of care distinguishes the ethical transgressor from the nihilist. To cheat in good faith, if such a thing is possible, is to act without contempt. The discreet lover who returns home more affectionate, attentive, and alive has, paradoxically, preserved care within betrayal. By contrast, the infidel who grows cruel, careless, or indifferent after the act has committed the deeper sin—the betrayal not of a promise but of concern itself.

3. Secrecy — Discretion or Deceit

Secrecy is unavoidable; deception is not. The line between them is the measure of conscience. Discretion conceals to protect tenderness; deceit conceals to protect the ego. Ethical secrecy requires discipline—the effort to minimize harm, to avoid flaunting or confessing what would destroy without healing. As in

111

diplomacy, the quiet lie may keep peace where a reckless truth would start a war. The moral question is whether silence serves love or merely shields vanity.

4. Duration — Moment or Double Life

Time converts lapse into pattern. A single breach, contained and acknowledged inwardly, may function as crisis and renewal—a lightning flash that clarifies what one still values. But repetition becomes structure, and structure becomes deceit. The ongoing affair that demands sustained performance corrupts the self; it splits attention and identity, leaving neither relationship intact. Ethical infidelity, if it exists at all, depends on brevity: the capacity to stop before self-duplication hardens into habit.

5. Power — Equality or Exploitation

Not all affairs occur on even ground. When hierarchy enters—employer and employee, mentor and student, celebrity and admirer—the moral calculus darkens. What looks like mutual consent may mask coercion; what looks like passion may be dependency disguised. The higher the asymmetry, the lower the ethical defensibility. The true test of power is whether both parties remain free to leave without penalty. If they cannot, the encounter is not erotic but economic.

6. Consequence — What the Act Leaves Behind

Every act leaves a residue. The final axis is not intention but outcome: did the trespass deepen understanding or merely scatter wreckage? Did it reanimate affection, or did it inaugurate mistrust? Consequence is where the moral and the pragmatic converge, where philosophy meets the household. In this domain, utilitarianism regains its dignity: sometimes the goodness of an act lies not in its purity but in its aftermath.

These six axes—intent, care, secrecy, duration, power, consequence—compose the moral geometry of infidelity. They are less commandments than coordinates, tracing the tension between freedom and fidelity that defines every human bond. Each subsequent section of this chapter will plot one region of that map: from the bounded, disciplined affair that preserves equilibrium, to the compulsive libertinism that annihilates it.

The Bounded Affair — Discretion and Containment

Every moral map has its gentlest terrain. In the geography of betrayal, that place is occupied by what might be called the *bounded affair*— an act of trespass contained by care, measured by restraint, and guided by an ethic of discretion. It is the rare instance where infidelity resembles a form of craftsmanship: deliberate, precise, and disciplined. The moral claim of the bounded affair is not innocence but proportion — that, like a controlled burn in a forest, it prevents a greater conflagration.

The essence of the bounded affair is *containment*. It is finite in scope, private in knowledge, and modest in ambition. It seeks renewal without revolution. The participants understand, tacitly or explicitly, that the relationship exists to relieve pressure, not to replace foundations. The lover is not a rival spouse but a temporary confidant, a mirror held up to a part of the self that daily life suppresses. When handled with restraint, such a connection may restore equilibrium rather than destroy it. It becomes, paradoxically, a gesture of preservation disguised as rebellion.

Discretion is the form that care takes here. The bounded affair's morality lies not in transparency but in tact. It avoids public discovery, not out of cowardice, but because revelation would convert a private therapy into a social catastrophe. The ethical infidel keeps the secret not to deny responsibility but to protect meaning. In this sense, secrecy functions as mercy — the small lie that spares needless pain. What separates discretion from deceit is intention: the former shields love; the latter evades it.

113

History and literature are full of such quiet transgressions. In Greene's *The End of the Affair*, the lovers' secrecy is heavy with moral tension yet driven by tenderness rather than cruelty. Somerset Maugham's world of diplomats and exiles understood this ethic instinctively: the elegant discretion that allowed flawed men and women to stumble, sin, and still keep their families intact. Even Flaubert, who condemned Emma Bovary's ruin, recognized the longing for transcendence that animates the well-contained trespass — the wish not to destroy life but to feel it again.

In psychological terms, the bounded affair often functions as *self-regulation*. It interrupts monotony, restores vitality, and diffuses resentment that might otherwise curdle into contempt within the marriage. The encounter — sometimes a single night, sometimes a short-lived liaison — becomes a reset: the forbidden taste that reminds one of appetite, the brief reminder that one is still capable of wanting and being wanted. If it ends as it should, with gratitude rather than attachment, the home to which one returns feels less like a cage and more like a choice.

Of course, the danger lies precisely in believing that containment can be guaranteed. Passion has a way of defying the boundaries we set for it. The ethical justification of the bounded affair depends on self-limitation — on the capacity to draw a line and keep it. Once emotion spills beyond that line, what was therapeutic becomes corrosive. To walk this narrow path demands moral intelligence, self-awareness, and a certain tragic humility: the knowledge that one is fallible, and that pleasure untethered from care quickly turns to harm.

If there is a virtue here, it is temperance — that ancient discipline Aristotle praised as the balance between indulgence and denial. The bounded affair neither idolizes abstinence nor glorifies excess. It accepts desire as a fact of being and seeks to manage it without cruelty. It is, at its best, an act of damage control, a quiet negotiation between human frailty and social necessity.

To call such an affair *ethical* is to recognize its motive: not conquest, not deceit for its own sake, but preservation — of affection, of sanity, of the fragile order that love builds against time. The bounded affair is the mercy of the small lie, the rebellion in service of peace. It keeps faith with the spirit of fidelity by breaking its letter carefully.

The Entangled Affair — Emotion, Confusion, and Drift

If the bounded affair is an art of limits, the entangled affair is the slow forgetting of them. It begins with the same ingredients— loneliness, curiosity, the wish to feel alive—but loses the discipline that once kept desire in proportion. What was meant as a contained spark becomes an alternate life. The self, once divided by choice, becomes divided by accident.

Entanglement creeps rather than crashes. It starts with a second conversation after the rendezvous, a text sent in the quiet hour before sleep, a secret wish that the other might understand what one's partner no longer does. The ethical infidel, once careful to protect the centre, begins to orbit elsewhere. The secrecy that was mercy turns to duplicity; the discretion that was tact becomes concealment; the renewal that once sustained the marriage starts to drain it.

Psychologically, this drift marks the point where eros outgrows its purpose. What began as vitality therapy transforms into dependence. The lover becomes not a mirror but a sanctuary, the place where one feels whole because one no longer feels responsible. It is at this stage that many adulterers begin to speak of destiny, of "soulmates," of cosmic justification. The language of ethics gives way to metaphysics, and self-deception blooms under the name of love.

Art has charted this terrain with ruthless accuracy. Emma Bovary's infatuation with her successive lovers is not lust but longing for significance; each encounter enlarges her emptiness. Anna Karenina's passion for Vronsky consumes her precisely because it refuses containment—she must either abolish her old world or live in unbearable contradiction. In the television series *The Affair*, the narrators retell the same events from incompatible perspectives, showing how entanglement warps perception itself: every desire becomes self-justifying, every hurt magnified.

The moral character of the entangled affair lies in *drift*—the absence of will. One does not decide to betray further; one simply continues. Routine replaces reflection, and what was once a transgression becomes a parallel domesticity, complete with tenderness, boredom, and lies. The ethical self dissolves into roles: spouse in one world, lover in another, both sincere, both untrue.

If the bounded affair demanded temperance, the entangled affair demands tragedy. It is here that conscience awakens late, recognizing that no choice will be clean. To end the affair is to wound the person who has become a second truth; to continue it is to hollow out the first. The result is often paralysis: the adulterer oscillates between confessions, making half-promises to both sides while believing he serves honesty.

Yet even here, all is not moral ruin. The pain of entanglement sometimes produces clarity unavailable to those who never stray. In being torn between two loves, one learns how desire can masquerade as salvation and how every freedom creates new dependencies. The insight costs dearly, but it can ripen into wisdom if it leads to renunciation—not the puritan's denial, but the adult's acceptance that one cannot be infinite.

The entangled affair therefore marks the border between *ethical* and *unethical* infidelity. On one side lies renewal through discretion; on the other, the slow corrosion of integrity through excess of feeling. What distinguishes them is not sex or secrecy but control—the capacity to end what must end. When that capacity fails, the infidel ceases to cheat in good faith and begins merely to drift.

Excellent — that's exactly the kind of cultural grounding this section needs. Japan provides an important counterpoint: a society where transactional intimacy is ritualized and socially contained rather than pathologized — and thus reveals how "cheating" is not a universal moral category, but a cultural construction tied to ideas of love, selfhood, and gender.

The Transactional "Betrayal" — Commodification and Escape

In the modern marketplace of desire, the line between fidelity and transgression blurs most visibly in the transactional encounter. Here, intimacy is mediated by money — the oldest lubricant of discretion. Whether it takes the form of a visit to a sex worker, an escort dinner, a massage parlour, or an online subscription, the transaction offers what relationships rarely can: clarity. Terms are set, expectations managed, feelings bracketed. No promises, no futures, no confessions — just an exchange of time, attention, and the brief illusion of connection.

To call this *betrayal* is already to assume that sex and love are indivisible. But for many, especially within long-term monogamy, they are not. The transactional encounter can function less as infidelity than as *maintenance* — a controlled outlet that relieves pressure without emotional fallout. The moral landscape here depends not on the act itself but on its *function*. Does it desecrate, or does it preserve? Does it diminish affection at home, or protect it from depletion?

In this sense, the sex worker occupies a curious ethical position in the emotional economy of marriage. Unlike the entangled lover, she asks for nothing beyond the agreed exchange; her role, paradoxically, may protect both client and spouse from deeper deceit. Historically, bourgeois societies understood this uncomfortably well. The Victorian gentleman, hypocritical though he was, relied on discreet liaisons to preserve domestic harmony. The arrangement was corrupt in its gendered structure, but its underlying logic remains: contained transgression as social stabilizer.

Nowhere is this clearer than in Japan, where the commodification of intimacy is normalized, even ritualized. From *soaplands* and *kyabakura* (hostess bars) to *delivery health* services and love hotels, a vast semi-formal industry exists to offer precisely the kind of bounded release that Western moralities condemn. For many Japanese men, visiting such establishments is not considered "cheating" but a socially accepted form of stress relief — a maintenance of equilibrium, not a betrayal of love. What Western puritanism would call immorality, Japanese pragmatism treats as hygiene: an acknowledgment of the body's needs within a culture that otherwise prizes social harmony and self-restraint. The key is *containment*: so long as emotion does not intrude and discretion is maintained, the act is seen not as moral collapse but as practical necessity.

This cultural contrast reveals something profound about the moral construction of fidelity. What counts as "cheating" is not a universal truth but a reflection of deeper civilizational temperaments. In the West, where love is psychologized and intimacy is supposed to unify body, soul, and truth, transactional sex feels like desecration — the reduction of the sacred to the purchasable. In Japan, where social order depends on managed outlets for human frailty, transactional intimacy serves the opposite function: it protects the sacred by quarantining the profane.

Our own moment, globalized and digital, has extended that Japanese logic without admitting it. Platforms like OnlyFans and cam sites transform desire into subscription: intimacy as service, affection as performance. The difference is no longer between paid and unpaid, but between *bounded fantasy* and *emotional leakage*. To pay for desire is not always to exploit; it may be to delineate. The ethical danger arises when transaction turns into obsession — when fantasy begins to replace rather than relieve reality, when the screen becomes sanctuary instead of supplement.

Philosophically, the transactional encounter tests the limits of what it means to cheat. If infidelity is the betrayal of emotional exclusivity, then sex without affection may not qualify. If it is the breach of bodily exclusivity, then even fantasy is suspect. Ethical judgment must therefore move beyond ontology—what "counts" as sex—to *telos*: what the act is for. In Aristotelian terms, an act that preserves equilibrium and relieves tension without cruelty may serve a higher moral purpose than a months-long flirtation sustained by lies.

To be clear, none of this sanctifies exploitation. Sex work is ethical only when chosen freely and practiced safely, when both parties remain autonomous and uncoerced. The moral failing lies not in the exchange but in the denial of recognition—when the client refuses to see the worker's humanity, or when the worker must efface her own to survive. But when both meet in understanding, the transaction can become something stranger and gentler: a brief, bounded theatre of compassion, in which two people enact need without illusion.

In this light, the "transactional betrayal" may belong squarely within the domain of *ethical infidelity*. It is discreet, contained, and — if pursued with respect — curiously honest about its limits. It acknowledges desire without confusing it for love. It may even protect love from exhaustion, from the crushing expectation that one person must fulfill every role — companion, muse, confessor, and cure. The sin, if there is one, lies not in the purchase but in the pretense that one has not purchased; not in the act, but in the shame that forces it underground.

Ethical infidelity in its transactional form thus asks for self-awareness, not purity. Desire, like money, can degrade or dignify depending on how it is spent. The transactional act, stripped of illusion, can become the most honest of all forms of cheating — the one that knows exactly what it is, and asks for nothing more.

The Serial Libertine — Compulsion and Narcissism

If the bounded affair is a moment of containment and the transactional act a controlled release, the serial libertine represents their unraveling. Here infidelity is no longer an episode but an identity. The lover's restlessness has hardened into rhythm; repetition replaces renewal. What once carried moral ambiguity now resembles addiction—an endless search for confirmation that never satisfies, because its object is not the other but the self.

The serial libertine mistakes conquest for connection. Each new partner becomes a mirror, reflecting back the illusion of potency and charm. What he desires is not intimacy but recognition: proof that he still commands attention, that his charisma has not decayed. The act of seduction becomes a ritual of self-reassurance. Once the mirror fades, he moves on, seeking another. The trail of discarded bodies and apologies that follows is not evidence of abundance but of emptiness—a hunger that feeds on its own echo.

In psychological terms, this pattern fuses libido with narcissism. The libido seeks life; narcissism seeks applause. The libertine confuses affirmation with affection, mistaking the charge of novelty for the spark of meaning. He cannot rest because stillness feels like annihilation. Each new liaison delays the confrontation with finitude—the knowledge that desire, like youth, has limits. Beneath the glamour of constant movement lies dread: the fear of being ordinary, of not being seen.

Modern culture celebrates this pathology as charisma. The playboy, the seducer, the high-functioning adulterer: they populate our screens as avatars of vitality. Don Draper in *Mad Men*, Tony Stark before his redemption arc, Casanova recast as lifestyle brand.

Yet their confidence conceals fatigue. Don Draper's revolving door of lovers never fills the void left by his own self-invention; each affair re-enacts his trauma rather than resolving it. The libertine lives in perpetual prologue—every beginning promising the transcendence that every ending denies.

Philosophically, the libertine embodies the corruption of freedom. Where the ethical infidel transgresses in order to return, the libertine transgresses to avoid returning at all. His "freedom" is flight: liberation without purpose, autonomy without depth. Nietzsche warned of this when he described the *last man*, blinking and smirking, forever chasing small pleasures to avoid despair. The libertine's joy is performative; his ecstasies are the exhaustion of a creature who has turned desire into labor.

This compulsive repetition also carries a social cost. The serial adulterer converts people into resources: emotional labor outsourced, intimacy consumed like a commodity. The ethical core of infidelity—self-awareness, proportion, care—evaporates. What remains is appetite as ideology. The libertine is capitalism's erotic citizen: endlessly circulating, terrified of attachment, measuring freedom in options. He calls this authenticity, but it is merely mobility without meaning.

To call such behavior "unethical infidelity" is not moralizing; it is diagnostic. The libertine's transgression lacks both restraint and reverence. He cheats not in good faith but in bad infinity—multiplying encounters to avoid introspection. There is no art in his betrayal, no dialectic between duty and desire. Only consumption.

Still, even this figure teaches something. He exposes what happens when the principle of renewal, so central to ethical infidelity, is divorced from reflection. He is the negative image of the careful adulterer—the warning that vitality without conscience collapses into compulsion. The libertine's tragedy is not that he cannot love others, but that he cannot stop performing love long enough to be loved.

Ethical infidelity begins with humility—the recognition that one's desires must be governed. The libertine's creed is pride: that his desires are their own justification. Where the ethical adulterer sins and returns wiser, the libertine sins and calls it enlightenment. His punishment is repetition.

The "Merciful Lie" — Cheating That Saves

There are betrayals that destroy, and there are betrayals that preserve. Between these poles lies the "merciful lie" — the transgression committed not for conquest or escape, but to keep something else alive. It is perhaps the most scandalous form of ethical infidelity: the act that wounds the law in order to protect the spirit that gave rise to it.

The merciful lie begins where communication has failed. A marriage hardened by habit, a partner withdrawn by illness, a life shrunken by duty — in such landscapes, desire does not vanish, it stagnates. The ethical question is not whether one should want, but what to do with wanting when there is no longer room for it to be safely spoken. Some confront it directly, and destroy the peace that remains; others repress it, and grow bitter. The merciful lie offers a third path: to seek release discreetly, to return home softer, calmer, more capable of affection.

In this moral grammar, the "cheat" becomes caretaker. The trespass, paradoxically, sustains the very relationship it violates. The lover outside the marriage becomes a pressure valve, not a rival. The small betrayal saves the larger promise. The partner who strays and returns with tenderness has sinned in form but acted in substance to preserve love's atmosphere.

Literature has hinted at this paradox for centuries, but rarely spoken it aloud. In Tolstoy's *Family Happiness*, an early, lesser-known work, a woman married to an older man discovers that love's maturity feels like loss — and quietly confesses to having loved someone else "only to know I could return." In Greene's novels, a brief affair often restores the moral seriousness of faith. Even in popular culture — say, the unspoken understanding between Tony Soprano and Carmela — we sense that some betrayals are tacitly absorbed into the moral economy of marriage, neither condoned nor condemned, but recognized as part of the cost of endurance.

The moral core of the merciful lie is intention. It demands that the transgressor act not from resentment, but from restraint; not to humiliate, but to preserve. Its ethics are consequentialist but delicate: the act is good only if it works — only if it returns the actor to the home with greater care, never discovered, never flaunted, and never repeated for sport. It is the ethic of triage: faced with the imperfection of all available options, one chooses the least cruel.

This is why discretion is non-negotiable. The merciful lie is moral only in its silence. The moment of confession transforms care into cruelty, turning a private act of maintenance into a public wound. The ethical infidel bears the burden of secrecy as a form of responsibility. What was meant to protect love must remain invisible to succeed.

Philosophically, this form of infidelity echoes the tragic ethics of necessity found in classical drama. In Euripides or Sophocles, the hero sins not because he despises the law, but because the law is inadequate to life's complexity. The merciful lie is born of the same predicament: the collision between fidelity as rule and fidelity as care. The act violates the first to preserve the second.

This, too, has its gendered history. For centuries, women have been expected to forgive men's discretions as "biological inevitabilities," while their own were treated as moral collapse. Yet the logic of the merciful lie may belong equally, perhaps even more powerfully, to women — to those who have long practiced emotional diplomacy to keep households intact. The ethical recognition here is that love, unlike law, cannot survive without adaptation; that sometimes, to remain faithful to the feeling, one must betray the form.

There is risk, of course. Every lie carries within it the seed of exposure. But to live entirely without secrecy is to live without depth. The merciful lie accepts this risk as the price of moral adulthood. It is not a model to emulate lightly, but a fact of the human heart to be understood: that sometimes, what looks like betrayal is a form of care too complex to name.

The merciful lie stands, then, as the highest and most precarious point in the taxonomy of ethical infidelity — the final border before morality tips into ruin. It is where intention and outcome align, however briefly, to create a fragile grace: the trespass that sustains, the sin that protects, the betrayal that saves.

The Confession Catastrophe

If the merciful lie represents the art of concealment in service of care, the confession catastrophe is its moral inversion — the belief that truth, once spoken, will heal what secrecy has harmed. It is the creed of our therapeutic age: that honesty is always good, that transparency redeems all sins, that light purifies. Yet in love, as in politics, exposure is not the same as justice. Some truths illuminate; others simply burn.

The impulse to confess is powerful because it feels virtuous. The guilty partner imagines that revelation will cleanse the conscience, restore equality, or rebuild trust. In reality, confession often transfers suffering rather than alleviates it. The weight of remorse is offloaded from the betrayer to the betrayed. What began as the adulterer's attempt at moral repair becomes, for the partner, a permanent wound. The need to "come clean" frequently masks a subtler narcissism: the wish to feel good again, even at another's expense.

Our culture has sanctified this impulse. The language of therapy and self-help teaches that "radical honesty" is the foundation of intimacy, that secrets corrode love from within. Yet psychoanalysis, that older and wiser discourse of the self, warns otherwise. Not all truths are assimilable; some destroy the psychic structure that makes love possible. As Freud observed, civilization depends on repression — on the modest concealments that prevent chaos. To remove every veil is not enlightenment; it is exposure.

In the confessional ethic of modern relationships, silence becomes the new sin. Couples are told that anything unsaid is a betrayal in waiting. The result is a kind of emotional surveillance state — an endless audit of motives, impulses, and histories. Love becomes less a sanctuary than an interrogation. In such climates, desire shrivels, not because it has vanished, but because it is too closely monitored to breathe.

Art has dramatized the disaster of confession with tragic precision. In Bergman's *Scenes from a Marriage*, the husband's revelation of an affair — intended as a bid for authenticity — shatters the couple's carefully built peace. What follows is not catharsis but disintegration: years of recrimination, shame, and futile reunion. In the American remake, the dynamic is reversed but the outcome identical; honesty yields no freedom, only fatigue. In *The Sopranos*, Tony's partial admissions to Carmela and to Dr. Melfi generate pity, not transformation; he remains trapped in the same repetitions, his confession another mask of control.

The ethical mistake underlying the confession catastrophe is the confusion of guilt with responsibility. Guilt seeks relief; responsibility seeks repair. Guilt says, *I must tell you so I can breathe again*. Responsibility says, *I must carry this so you don't have to*. The merciful liar chooses the latter. Their silence is not denial but discipline — a refusal to turn private weakness into collective pain.

To be sure, secrecy can curdle into deceit. The difference lies in purpose. Concealment that protects tenderness is not the same as concealment that enables cruelty. The moral challenge is to discern which kind one practices. But confession, pursued as an end in itself, abdicates that discernment; it mistakes speaking for healing. The result is moral exhibitionism: the spectacle of sincerity that sacrifices intimacy to absolution.

Philosophically, this reveals a tension between two moral traditions. The Christian lineage prizes confession as the path to grace; the classical tradition, from Aristotle to Montaigne, prizes discretion as the mark of maturity. The first seeks purity through speech; the second, harmony through measure. Our culture, having inherited both, cannot decide whether to tell or to protect — and so it tells compulsively, even when protection would be kinder.

The truth is that love, like art, depends on shadows. Every enduring relationship contains an inner chamber of silence — not deceit, but privacy; not evasion, but tact. To abolish that space is to destroy the conditions for curiosity and forgiveness alike. The confession catastrophe unfolds when we mistake that space for hypocrisy, when we forget that the ability to keep a secret is not a sign of moral failure but of emotional restraint.

In the age of radical transparency, ethical infidelity therefore makes a subversive claim: that sometimes silence is the higher truth, and that to lie with care may be more moral than to confess without it. The merciful lie preserves the world; the confession catastrophe ends it.

The Spectrum Summarized — From Vice to Virtue

Every moral order is a hierarchy, even when it pretends to be neutral. To think ethically about infidelity is to reintroduce hierarchy where moral panic once reigned — not to justify betrayal, but to rank its forms by intention, care, and consequence. What emerges from the preceding typology is not a defense of all transgression, but an anatomy of its differences: a spectrum that runs from the destructive to the restorative, from vice to something approaching virtue.

At the lowest end of that spectrum lies the *serial libertine*. His infidelity is not an act but a habit — the pursuit of affirmation without empathy, desire as domination, sex as consumption. Here, cheating becomes indistinguishable from exploitation. The narcissism that drives him is not passion but self-avoidance, a restless defense against his own emptiness. His is not the freedom of Eros but the fatigue of appetite. It is, in every moral sense, a failure of attention.

Slightly higher, but still within the territory of vice, lies the *entangled affair*. Its sin is confusion rather than cruelty. The transgressor here is sincere but unmoored, overwhelmed by emotion that outgrows its discretion. Love, when mixed with self-deception, becomes tyranny in soft form: the desire to escape responsibility in the name of authenticity. Yet, unlike the libertine, the entangled adulterer is capable of remorse — and, therefore, redemption. His tragedy is that he mistakes passion for purpose.

Between these darker forms and the more disciplined lies the *transactional betrayal*. Its moral neutrality depends on context: exploitative when one-sided, almost therapeutic when mutual. Where affection is not demanded and autonomy is preserved, the exchange can serve equilibrium rather than erode it. It is neither virtue nor vice, but a pragmatic compromise — a reminder that the body, too, has its politics of care. Japan's normalization of such encounters reflects not amorality but an advanced ethics of containment: a recognition that human frailty can be managed without moral hysteria.

Ascending the spectrum, we reach the *bounded affair*. Here, the elements of ethical infidelity first appear. The trespass is contained, self-aware, and motivated by preservation rather than conquest. Its secrecy is not deceit but tact; its risk is calculated, its harm minimized. The bounded affair violates the law to uphold the spirit — a disciplined transgression whose purpose is equilibrium. It is the act of a person who knows what they endanger and who stops before the edge.

Beyond this lies the *merciful lie* — the summit of ethical infidelity. It is the betrayal that saves: the discreet, compassionate deception that keeps love alive when honesty would destroy it. Its morality lies entirely in its motive and execution. Done without cruelty, flaunting, or repetition, it becomes the purest expression of the paradox at the heart of human relationships: that truth and tenderness sometimes diverge. It is the Aristotelian *phronesis* — practical wisdom — applied to the domain of intimacy.

The opposite pole of that wisdom is the *confession catastrophe*. It is not an affair, but an ethic — one that mistakes transparency for virtue and catharsis for care. If the merciful lie preserves the bond through silence, the confession catastrophe destroys it through honesty. It reveals that even the moral impulse, when absolutized, can turn cruel. Between these extremes, discretion emerges as the golden mean — neither the lie of indifference nor the violence of full disclosure.

What this taxonomy reveals is that the ethics of infidelity are not defined by action alone, but by *orientation*. The crucial question is not, "Did you stray?" but, "What did your straying serve?" When transgression serves the ego, it is vice; when it serves vitality without cruelty, it becomes forgivable; when it serves love itself, it approaches grace.

To recognize these gradations is not to weaken morality, but to humanize it. Absolute purity, like absolute corruption, belongs to angels and monsters — not to us. Most human beings live somewhere between the two, improvising small moral economies of care, guilt, and restraint. The taxonomy of cheating, properly understood, is not a map of sin, but a chart of sympathy. It teaches that the same act can be vicious in one heart and merciful in another — that what redeems is not conduct alone, but conscience.

The Gray Ethics of Love

Every moral vocabulary must, sooner or later, admit the color gray. Purity and depravity are the easy categories — they flatter the mind with certainty. But life, particularly in matters of the heart, is composed of intermediate hues: of care entangled with deceit, of desire alloyed with duty, of tenderness that wounds in order to heal. To live morally within that spectrum is to abandon the dream of innocence and replace it with the discipline of nuance.

The taxonomy we have traced reveals that infidelity is not one thing but many: vice when thoughtless, mercy when careful, destruction when flaunted, and sometimes, paradoxically, preservation when hidden. To speak of *ethical cheating* is not to romanticize betrayal, but to name a reality that moral absolutism cannot comprehend: that people fail each other constantly, and yet love continues. The real task is not to abolish contradiction, but to navigate it without cruelty.

In this light, the mature ethic of love is not purity but *proportion*. It asks of us not perfection, but vigilance — the ongoing effort to measure impulse against care, freedom against responsibility. Ethics begins when appetite is joined to attention. It is what separates the merciful liar from the libertine, the discreet adulterer from the narcissist, the thoughtful transgressor from the compulsive. The difference is not what they do, but how and why they do it.

This is the moral adulthood that modern relationships so often lack: the acceptance that goodness is not the absence of failure, but its management. To love well, one must know one's limits, one's hungers, and one's capacity for harm. Pretending otherwise is not virtue but denial. Infidelity, when viewed without panic, simply reveals this truth in sharper relief. It is not a disease to be eradicated, but a human condition to be understood — the shadow cast by our yearning for both stability and transcendence.

The lesson of the gray ethics of love is humility. Every long relationship will, at some point, face temptation, boredom, resentment, or neglect. The question is not whether these will come, but how they will be borne. Some will respond with cruelty disguised as honesty; others with silence that corrodes. A few will respond with tact — the quiet intelligence that knows when to speak and when to protect, when to seek release and when to return. In this tact lies the germ of what might, without irony, be called ethical infidelity.

For those who live by that ethic, morality is not a code but a craft. It requires judgment, timing, proportion — a sense of what the situation can bear. There are no rules, only principles: restraint, respect, care, and the humility to stop before the act becomes vanity. To cheat ethically is, above all, to cheat *consciously* — to do so in good faith, with full awareness of the risks and responsibilities that accompany desire.

That, then, is where our inquiry must go next. Having mapped the moral terrain of infidelity — its degrees, its dangers, its justifications — we must now descend from theory to practice. If such a thing as ethical cheating exists, how might it actually be done? What forms of vigilance, restraint, and self-knowledge does it require? What principles can protect the heart from collapsing into hypocrisy or harm?

The next chapter offers no permission, only preparation. It is a guide for those who will fail, but who wish to fail well — a manual for sinners who still believe in love.

Chapter 8:
How to Cheat (Ethically)

The Scandal of Practical Ethics

There is something obscene about writing a guide to cheating. To offer *rules* for betrayal feels like a moral perversion — the corruption of ethics by cunning. Yet every society, even the most sanctimonious, quietly depends on such rules. People fail each other constantly; the only question is whether they do so with grace or with carnage. What follows, then, is not a license to sin, but an attempt to reduce the collateral damage of human nature.

To speak of *ethical infidelity* is already to scandalize. Ethics, after all, is supposed to restrain desire, not refine it. But perhaps that distinction is itself the problem. The moral tradition that equates virtue with repression has failed us; it has produced neither saints nor stability, only hypocrisy and boredom. What is needed is not the abolition of ethics, but its reconfiguration — a moral vocabulary that can accommodate failure without collapsing into cynicism.

This is the scandal of practical ethics: that the most important moral questions are not about purity, but about proportion. How much risk can love bear? How much truth can kindness survive? How much deceit can care contain before it curdles into cruelty? We are trained to believe that ethics is a matter of commandments. In truth, it is a matter of calibration — of tact, timing, and judgment. It is not a science but an art, and like all arts, it has its techniques.

To codify those techniques is not to celebrate transgression but to acknowledge its inevitability. Infidelity is not a modern invention; it is as old as pair-bonding itself. What is modern is our insistence on narrating it through purity and confession — the endless psychodrama of guilt and disclosure that leaves no space for discretion, no dignity for failure. A mature ethics must do better. It must ask not merely *whether* we err, but *how* we err — and whether we can do so without destroying what remains worth saving.

This, then, is a manual not for libertines, but for adults: for those who recognize that love is fragile, that desire is unruly, and that fidelity, like democracy, survives only through continual maintenance. To cheat ethically is not to abolish conscience, but to refine it. It means to fail intelligently, with awareness and restraint — to trespass in good faith.

If this offends moral absolutists, so much the better. Absolutism is the luxury of those who have never faced temptation, or whose failures have remained conveniently invisible. The rest of us must make do with ambiguity — with the slow, patient work of harm reduction in the realm of the heart. The rules that follow are not commandments but coordinates: principles of discretion, proportion, and care.

They are addressed not to the cynic, but to the contrite; not to the predator, but to the conflicted; not to those who mock love, but to those who wish to preserve it from their own imperfection.

To cheat ethically is to begin from humility: the recognition that one will fail, and that failure, properly managed, need not destroy.

The First Commandment — Know Why You're Doing It

Before any act becomes ethical, it must first become conscious. Most betrayals begin not in malice but in confusion — the slow drift of an unexamined need. To cheat ethically, if such a phrase can mean anything, is to cheat with clarity. The first commandment, then, is simple but merciless: *know why you're doing it.*

Desire is rarely what it claims to be. The affair pursued in the name of passion may conceal loneliness. The flirtation justified as freedom may mask fear. Many adulterers mistake restlessness for vitality, or boredom for moral awakening. They tell themselves they seek love, when in truth they are fleeing routine, grief, or the humiliation of aging. The ethical infidel must strip away these disguises. Before acting, one must ask: *What hunger am I trying to feed?*

Philosophy offers few better tools than this question. The Stoics would have called it the work of distinguishing impressions from reality — of knowing which desires are truly ours, and which are reactions to pain. Freud, less stoic, saw affairs as eruptions of the repressed self — the unconscious staging a revolt against a life grown too rigid. Both were right. But awareness does not guarantee justification; it only grants lucidity. To understand one's motive is not to absolve it, but to see it nakedly enough to choose responsibly.

Ethical infidelity demands this kind of moral x-ray. One must trace the chain of causation inward: Is this act an expression of love's exhaustion or of one's own? Is it a search for novelty, or for recognition? Will it serve vitality, or vanity? The adulterer who cannot answer these questions with honesty should not proceed. Not because cheating is wicked, but because thoughtlessness is.

It is here that the difference between *escape* and *renewal* begins. Escape seeks erasure — the fantasy of another life, another self.

Renewal seeks re-entry — the temporary widening of experience that allows one to return with clearer eyes. The first is cowardice dressed as courage; the second, at least potentially, a form of moral realism. Ethical infidelity belongs only to the latter.

A useful test helps draw the line. Ask yourself: *If no one could ever know — if there were no secrecy to savor, no rule to break, no revenge to stage — would I still want this?* If the answer is yes, perhaps your desire carries truth in it. If the answer is no, then the affair is not about love at all; it is about performance — the narcissistic thrill of rebellion for its own sake.

Slavoj Žižek once joked that when an affair ends a marriage, it ends the affair too — because what made it thrilling was precisely that it was forbidden. Once it becomes legitimate, it loses its charge. The insight is cruel but true: many adulterers do not crave another person so much as they crave the *drama* of transgression. Their pleasure depends on the existence of the very law they violate. Ethical infidelity, by contrast, seeks renewal rather than spectacle. It does not need to destroy in order to feel alive.

This inner accounting is not puritanism; it is preparation. Every ethical transgression must begin with confession — not to one's partner, but to oneself. The adulterer who understands their motive can contain it; the one who lies to themselves will lie to everyone. Moral intelligence begins in self-suspicion.

The point is not to justify infidelity with eloquent motives, but to ensure that the act arises from something more than impulse. There are many bad reasons to cheat — resentment, boredom, narcissism — and only a few good ones, all of them connected to the desire to feel *alive* without cruelty. To know the difference is the first discipline of conscience.

If ethics begins in awareness, then every ethical affair begins before it happens — in the silence of self-examination. It is not a question of permission but of proportion: the effort to ensure that what one seeks is truly worth what one risks.

The next rule, then, follows naturally: if the *why* is clear, the *how* must be contained. To act without boundaries is to destroy the very thing one hoped to preserve.

The Rule of Containment — Keep It Bounded

If the first rule of ethical infidelity is to know why, the second is to know where it ends. Ethics, like art, depends on form. An affair without limits is not liberation but drift — an attempt to build infinity out of appetite. The ethical adulterer, by contrast, lives within a self-imposed boundary. They understand that what gives an act moral shape is not its permission but its proportion.

Containment is the difference between fire and arson. Desire, like flame, gives warmth and light only when held in place. Left unchecked, it consumes indiscriminately. The purpose of containment is not repression but preservation: to ensure that the transgression serves vitality rather than chaos.

This means establishing boundaries that are both practical and moral. Keep it separate from the life you intend to protect — emotionally, geographically, even temporally. The affair that creeps into the daily world, that demands constant communication, that begins to shape the rhythms of ordinary life, is already losing its ethical character. The goal is not to build a second life but to preserve the integrity of the first.

In this sense, ethical infidelity is closer to ritual than romance. It is an interval — a suspension of the ordinary, governed by its own rules, existing precisely because it is temporary. It must remain discreet, self-contained, and finite. The adulterer who promises more than this, who begins to conflate their lover with salvation, has already betrayed the very restraint that makes their transgression bearable.

This does not mean cynicism. To treat the other person as mere instrument — a vessel for release, a toy of ego — is not ethical but cruel. Containment requires a double awareness: care for the other's dignity without allowing the affair to endanger the lives it was meant to protect. The ethical infidel must balance tenderness with discipline. They must know how to draw the curtain gently, to end without wreckage.

The ancient philosophers would have understood this. Aristotle taught that virtue lies in the mean — between excess and deficiency. The Stoics, again, insisted that freedom is not the absence of constraint but mastery over impulse. Even Nietzsche, patron saint of transgression, warned that "he who fights monsters must see to it that he does not become one." The same rule applies here: to wander responsibly is to keep one's bearings.

Containment is not cowardice. It is the mark of seriousness. It acknowledges that the transgression is dangerous — that it could, if left unbounded, destroy everything that gave it meaning. The ethical adulterer accepts this risk not as an excuse for recklessness, but as a reason for caution. Their discretion is not shame but care; their silence, not deceit but stewardship.

In this light, secrecy is not only strategic but moral. The point is not merely to avoid discovery but to protect everyone involved from unnecessary pain. The affair that remains contained — emotionally modest, logistically separate, and self-aware — can function as an act of renewal. The affair that spills into entanglement becomes indistinguishable from betrayal.

There is a Japanese proverb that captures this balance: *"The nail that sticks out gets hammered down."* In Japan, where certain forms of sex work are normalized as we have already observed, the distinction between the private and the illicit is handled with quiet pragmatism. A husband who visits a hostess bar or an escort may not be condemned, provided he keeps his obligations intact. What matters is not the act but its discipline — that it restores harmony rather than disrupts it. Ethical infidelity, at its best, follows a similar logic: not indulgence without end, but the maintenance of equilibrium through controlled transgression.

The measure of an ethical affair, then, is not intensity but containment. It should end before it begins to expand, before longing hardens into dependency or guilt curdles into resentment. The art lies in knowing when to stop — in understanding that a boundary willingly chosen is the most humane form of fidelity left to those who have already crossed the line.

The Rule of Care — Harm No One You Don't Have To

Every act of infidelity is, by definition, an injury. The question is not whether it hurts, but *how much* and *to whom*. Ethical infidelity does not pretend to erase the wound; it seeks to limit its spread. Its moral principle is triage: minimize casualties, spare the innocent, and protect those whose peace you still value.

To cheat carelessly is to turn longing into cruelty. The ethical adulterer must never humiliate, never flaunt, never convert private freedom into public spectacle. Even in transgression, there are duties. The first is toward the partner who remains at home — the person to whom one still owes tenderness, even if that tenderness has grown quiet. Their ignorance is not contempt but mercy: a protection against pain that serves no purpose.

The second duty is toward the lover themselves. Do not promise what cannot be given. Do not inflate a moment into a myth. Ethical infidelity requires honesty in proportion — not the honesty of confession, but the honesty of clarity. To offer affection without illusion is the only form of respect available in a situation built on contradiction. You cannot make everyone happy, but you can refuse to make anyone miserable.

This is what Spinoza might have called *benevolent realism*: the refusal to confuse compassion with sentimentality. To care, in this sense, is not to dramatize feeling but to contain it. Passion that destroys the world around it is not love but narcissism. Ethical infidelity, if it is to remain ethical at all, must preserve its humility: to know that one's desire, however powerful, is not an excuse for wreckage.

Ferrante's women understand this with brutal clarity. They live within contradictions — longing for freedom while bound by care, acting against others while trying not to harm them more than they must. Their moral intelligence lies not in innocence but in *measure*: the ability to hold conflicting truths without turning them into absolutes. In that sense, Ferrante's universe is the true landscape of ethical infidelity — one where love and damage coexist, and where the task is not to escape contradiction but to inhabit it well.

Care, here, is not sentiment but craft. It requires tact — the steady awareness of who might be touched by one's actions and how to keep that circle as small as possible. It means thinking ahead, not only about pleasure but aftermath. It means refusing to let the momentary eclipse the enduring.

The careless adulterer imagines that what happens in secret has no consequence; the careful one knows that every secret exerts pressure on the world. Their ethic is to distribute that pressure wisely — to shoulder more of it so that others feel less. To lie, in this sense, is not cowardice but service.

If ethical infidelity has a golden rule, it is this: *act as though everyone you love will someday have to live with what you have done — even if they never know it.* The affair must not only remain hidden; it must remain harmless. To achieve that is almost impossible, which is why it requires discipline, not license.

The next rule follows naturally from this one: care begins in silence. The truest act of protection is not a confession, but the mercy of withholding.

The Rule of Discretion — The Mercy of Silence

No affair remains ethical once exposed. Discovery converts ambiguity into cruelty: what was once a private negotiation between freedom and care becomes a public wound. The first duty of the ethical adulterer, therefore, is not to confess but to protect — to ensure that what has already risked too much does not injure further.

In the sentimental imagination, confession redeems. We are taught that honesty purifies, that to "come clean" is to restore integrity. But confession, in the context of infidelity, rarely serves truth; it serves the confessor. It lightens one's own conscience by transferring pain to another. To speak in order to be forgiven is to make the wounded party responsible for your healing. The ethical adulterer refuses this. They understand that the burden of silence is theirs to bear alone.

Silence, then, is not cowardice. It is the last service one can perform for those one still loves. It is a kind of moral labor — the quiet, ongoing work of protecting the very world one has endangered. This is what discretion means: not evasion but stewardship. The point is not to erase what happened, but to contain its consequences.

To lie well is to lie mercifully. It requires tact, proportion, and purpose. The ethical liar speaks only to preserve — to sustain the fabric of shared life, not to embellish it. They understand that truth, when unfiltered, can be an instrument of violence. Not all wounds need salt.

There is a difference between secrecy and deceit. Deceit is active — the manipulation of another's perception for gain.

Secrecy is protective — the withholding of what would only cause pain. To keep a secret well is to honor the distinction between what must be known and what must be borne.

Elena Ferrante's characters live by this wisdom. They understand that silence is not emptiness but form — the frame that gives intensity its dignity. In their world, revelation is rarely liberation; it is exposure, and exposure is dangerous. Their silences are not absence but endurance, acts of care performed in the negative space of speech. Ethical infidelity demands a similar restraint: to carry contradiction quietly, to resist the contemporary urge to narrate everything.

In an era that mistakes visibility for virtue, silence becomes an act of defiance. To remain opaque in a culture of self-disclosure is not dishonesty but dignity. The ethical adulterer, like any moral agent, must learn to distinguish between truth-telling that heals and truth-telling that destroys. The question is never *"Is this true?"* but *"Is this necessary?"*

To practice the mercy of silence is to accept that one's transgression will never be fully resolved, only managed. It is to live with the knowledge that the truth, if spoken, would turn a private failure into a collective tragedy. The ethical adulterer, in carrying this secret, takes on the full weight of responsibility — quietly, invisibly, without praise.

Discretion, then, is not only the continuation of care; it is its perfection. It transforms secrecy into tenderness, the unsaid into protection. It is the last refuge of love in a world that demands confession as spectacle.

The next rule turns from moral concealment to practical preservation. If one must sin discreetly, one must also do so safely — not only for the soul, but for the body and the world that sustains it.

The Rule of Safety — Protect Bodies and Reputations

Care and discretion mean little if one is reckless with the tangible. The first law of any transgression is containment; the second is hygiene. Ethical infidelity demands both. What is at stake is not only the heart but the body — and in the contemporary world, the digital body too.

To cheat ethically is to understand that every careless act multiplies risk. Passion cannot be an excuse for negligence. The moral and the physical are inseparable: a person who takes unnecessary chances with health, privacy, or reputation betrays not only their partner but the principle of stewardship itself.

Physical safety comes first. No affair, however discreet, remains ethical if it endangers anyone's health. Safe sex, contraception, and regular testing are not bureaucratic intrusions on intimacy; they are expressions of respect. They mark the difference between appetite and attention. To safeguard the body is to acknowledge that desire, while fleeting, lives in a world of consequence. Ethical infidelity demands the kind of maturity that refuses to outsource risk to others.

Reputational safety comes next. Every message, photo, or receipt is a potential weapon against dignity. In a culture where the private collapses into the public with a click, carelessness is not innocence — it is vanity. The ethical adulterer must treat technology as a moral landscape: no phones in vulnerable moments, no emails, no shared cloud, no traceable evidence of what should remain ephemeral. The test is simple: if discovery would humiliate someone you love, the act was not worth doing, and the proof not worth keeping.

Technology, once a tool for secrecy, has become its enemy. Desire leaves metadata; every whisper becomes a potential headline. To protect one's privacy is therefore an act of solidarity — not only with one's partner and lover but with all those whose

143

lives might be collateral damage in a scandal. Stewardship means anticipating how far a secret can travel once it escapes one's grasp, and ensuring it never begins that journey.

Safety also means emotional quarantine. No affair remains clean if it crosses into shared circles — colleagues, friends, neighbors. The overlap of worlds breeds chaos. Ethical infidelity, to stay ethical, must exist in a separate register of life: a sealed compartment, not a second home. The more porous the boundary, the greater the risk of contagion — gossip, envy, harm.

In this sense, caution is not cowardice but craft. It is the discipline of those who understand that even pleasure has an ecology — that love, like fire, must be tended carefully or it will consume indiscriminately. The Japanese call this sensibility *enryo*: restraint born of consideration. The restrained person does not suppress desire; they refine it until it burns clean.

The careless adulterer imagines themselves free; the careful one knows that freedom without precaution is another form of bondage. They practice the ethics of prevention — not out of paranoia, but out of respect for the fragile ecosystem of human connection.

To protect bodies and reputations is therefore to extend the logic of care to its outermost edge: to ensure that what began in secrecy does not end in ruin. The ethical adulterer must live as if their acts are already known, and yet behave so well that, even if discovered, they would not appear contemptible — only human.

The next rule carries this logic to its conclusion. If safety is about prevention, *return* is about renewal. The affair must end not in destruction but in restoration — a coming home wiser, cleaner, and more alive to the life one momentarily left.

The Rule of Return — Come Home Better

The final test of ethical infidelity is not whether it happened, but what it leaves behind. The act itself matters less than the return. The affair, if it is to mean anything beyond appetite, must end in renewal — a recovery of tenderness for the life one momentarily stepped outside.

To cheat ethically is to risk one's equilibrium for insight. The experience must not merely consume; it must teach. The moral criterion is simple: *if you do not come home better, you should not have left.*

The return is the hardest part, because it demands transformation without confession. You must carry the knowledge of what you have done without transferring the burden to those who should be spared it. The work of return is internal — to translate what was reckless into what is gentle, to turn what was selfish into gratitude.

Kazuo Ishiguro's *The Remains of the Day* offers a parable of this unspoken redemption. The butler Stevens, defined by a lifetime of restraint, spends his later years haunted by what never happened between himself and Miss Kenton. The unfulfilled desire becomes his education: in recognizing his repression, he also glimpses the cost of emotional cowardice. His unacted infidelity — the road never taken — restores his moral sight. He learns, too late, that love's grace lies not in possession but in attentiveness. Ethical infidelity demands the same lesson, though in reverse: to act without losing sight of what remains worth preserving.

The purpose of an affair, if it is to have one, is not escape but re-entry. The world outside the marriage — the forbidden space of otherness — should sharpen one's vision of what is already one's own. The ethical adulterer does not return home as penance but as fulfillment, carrying with them the proof that vitality still circulates beneath routine. To come home better is to recognize the ordinary again as miraculous.

Brief Encounter captures this poignantly. Two married strangers meet by chance, fall into an almost-affair, and then part without consummation. Their love is real, but its impossibility saves it. The renunciation itself becomes their redemption — not moralistic self-denial, but acknowledgment that what they have glimpsed must be folded back into the lives they have already built. It is one of cinema's rare depictions of fidelity regained through infidelity.

Coming home better means resisting two equal temptations: cynicism and sentimentality. The first says nothing matters; the second says everything does. The truth is quieter: that even a moral failure can widen one's capacity for understanding. The ethical adulterer returns not sanctified but softened, more patient, less vain — having learned that desire is not infinite, and that love's endurance depends on the careful tending of what already exists.

The return is also the final safeguard against delusion. The affair that continues to haunt or dominate has failed its purpose. What was meant as restoration has become repetition. Ethical infidelity must be metabolized into ordinary life — digested, not displayed. The lesson, once absorbed, becomes invisible.

To come home better is to make peace with contradiction — to realize that fidelity is not a state but a practice, renewed through failure. The one who returns wiser has not betrayed less, only understood more. In that understanding lies a strange form of purity: the knowledge that what makes love precious is its fragility, and that what endures is never innocence but care.

The next rule follows naturally: every renewal must stop short of re-enchantment. What was temporary must remain so. To mistake the lesson for a life is to let the lie become the truth — and that is the final, unforgivable collapse.

The Rule of Limits — Stop Before the Lie Becomes the Life

Every transgression begins as an adventure and ends as administration. The thrill of secrecy hardens into routine; the momentary becomes maintenance. What was once escape becomes a second cage. This is the natural entropy of desire — and the reason every ethical affair must contain its own ending.

The rule of limits is simple but brutal: stop before the lie becomes the life. The difference between an act of renewal and a life of deceit is timing. Ethical infidelity, by definition, must remain finite. Once it begins to require constant justification, once it demands coordination rather than concealment, once it becomes a *project*, it has ceased to be ethical.

The hardest thing for any lover to accept is that meaning depends on mortality. What gives the affair its moral force — its vitality, its capacity to restore perspective — is precisely that it cannot last. The finitude is what saves it from nihilism. To extend it indefinitely is to mistake freedom for dependency, to confuse what healed you for what defines you.

Milan Kundera understood this in *The Unbearable Lightness of Being*. Tomas, a man who believes in "erotic friendship" without emotional commitment, mistakes repetition for control. His affairs, at first acts of autonomy, multiply until they become indistinguishable from habit. He discovers, too late, that freedom without limit becomes its own burden — that what he called lightness was only another form of fatigue. His tragedy is not that he desired too much, but that he mistook motion for meaning.

The ethical adulterer must avoid Tomas's fate. They must treat desire as a season, not a climate. The very moment the secret begins to feel permanent — when it demands routine, attention, explanation — is the moment it should end. The moral climax of infidelity is not consummation but cessation. To stop is to reclaim sovereignty from compulsion.

Renunciation, in this light, is not repression but mastery. It transforms the act from indulgence into knowledge. To end deliberately is to preserve the dignity of what was momentary, to freeze it before decay sets in. This is why every ethical affair must be capable of ending with a single decision. If it cannot be closed, it was never truly yours; it owned you from the start.

Limits also protect truth from corrosion. The longer a lie endures, the more it demands maintenance, and the more it replaces reality with its imitation. The ethical adulterer must not allow deception to metastasize into identity. To live entirely within concealment is to become a fiction — and fictions, however seductive, cannot love.

Knowing when to stop is therefore the final act of care — care for oneself, for the lover, and for the partner at home. It is the moral climax of the entire enterprise. The affair that ends at the right time becomes memory, perhaps even meaning; the one that continues too long becomes ruin. The choice is between an elegy and an erosion.

Flaubert hinted at this in *Sentimental Education*. Frédéric Moreau's romantic idealism curdles into inertia because he cannot stop desiring what he never truly wanted. His failure is not excess passion, but the inability to let go. To cling to what has already fulfilled its purpose is to turn vitality into vanity.

The ethical adulterer, by contrast, knows that to end well is to love well. Their withdrawal is not cowardice but reverence — an acknowledgment that the boundary, once crossed, must eventually be restored. To step back across it is to honor the very structure that made the transgression meaningful.

The rule of limits, then, is the moral capstone of all the others. It is the moment when pleasure becomes understanding, and understanding becomes mercy. To stop before the lie becomes the life is to rescue desire from self-destruction and to return to the world, not innocent, but intact.

The next and final rule follows naturally: once the act is over, the burden remains. Ethical infidelity does not seek exoneration. Its last demand is responsibility — to carry the knowledge alone, without spectacle, without justification, and without asking to be understood.

The Rule of Responsibility — Carry the Weight Alone

Every act of transgression leaves residue — not evidence, perhaps, but weight. The ethical adulterer must learn to carry it. Once the act is done, there is no absolution waiting, no grand dialectical reconciliation between guilt and grace. What remains is the slow discipline of responsibility: to live with what one has chosen, quietly, without spectacle.

The temptation, once the danger has passed, is to seek understanding — to explain, to confess, to make the hidden known so that it can be forgiven. But this instinct is itself another form of vanity. The desire to be understood is the ego's last defense against consequence. The ethical adulterer refuses this consolation. They know that understanding, if it comes at the cost of another's peace, is not absolution but cruelty.

To carry the weight alone is not self-punishment. It is the final gesture of care. The one who has transgressed must take upon themselves the full burden of their freedom. This is what distinguishes ethical infidelity from ordinary betrayal: not that it avoids harm entirely, but that it refuses to distribute it. The pain belongs to the one who caused it; they must absorb it without making others their accomplices in remorse.

Kierkegaard called this solitude *the trial of the knight of faith*. The knight acts according to a private necessity that the world cannot

149

comprehend, and then accepts the silence that follows. He does not demand applause or absolution; he walks alone, answerable only to the inward judge. Ethical infidelity, too, demands this quiet integrity — to acknowledge that one's act, however sincere, cannot be universalized or explained. It must remain singular, secret, and borne in silence.

Carrying the weight also means resisting the twin temptations of cynicism and sentimentality. The cynic shrugs and says, "everyone cheats"; the sentimentalist weeps and seeks redemption. Both refuse the work of endurance. Responsibility is neither despair nor indulgence — it is the quiet middle path where one accepts imperfection as the price of freedom.

This solitude is not sterile. It can, paradoxically, deepen love. The one who carries their secret well becomes gentler, more aware of fragility — not because guilt ennobles, but because having touched the edge of destruction, they understand how much must be protected. This is the moral residue of ethical infidelity: the slow education in tenderness that comes from having survived one's own contradictions.

The adulterer who carries their secret badly infects everything around them: the sudden mood, the misplaced defensiveness, the need for reassurance. But the one who carries it well lets it sink quietly into their soul, where it becomes humility. They no longer seek to be good; they try, instead, to be kind.

To carry the weight alone is to reject both confession and denial — to accept that moral life is not a ledger of balances but a practice of bearing. The affair may have ended, but its consequence does not. The ethical adulterer continues to live with what they know, not as punishment, but as instruction.

The dignity of this solitude lies in its refusal of self-justification. The person who has cheated ethically does not claim that their act was right — only that they will bear its wrongness well. That is what makes it moral. They do not hide behind philosophy or psychology or the plea of biology. They simply stand inside their imperfection, without excuses.

In this way, responsibility becomes a form of grace. It turns the private weight of guilt into a kind of ballast — the thing that steadies the soul. To carry it well is to live without exoneration but also without despair, to make peace with the fact that human beings cannot be pure, only attentive.

The final movement of this book belongs to that grace — to the strange, redemptive beauty of failure itself.

Chapter 9:
Towards A Philosophy of Faithful Betrayals

Reframing the Question

We have spent this book circling what at first seemed a scandalous question: can one cheat ethically? But the deeper we go, the clearer it becomes that this question was never truly about cheating at all. It was about fidelity — not as obedience to a rule, but as a mode of life. The real problem is not how to avoid betrayal, but how to live meaningfully in the presence of it.

To ask whether cheating can be ethical is to expose the limits of our moral imagination. Most of our inherited ethics — religious, romantic, and liberal alike — assumes that fidelity means constancy, sameness, the refusal to deviate. But fidelity, properly understood, is not static. It is not the preservation of form but the renewal of commitment through time. What we call "betrayal" is often only the visible trace of that renewal: the moment when the old form cracks to reveal a deeper continuity beneath.

Faithfulness, in this sense, is not purity but *attunement*. It is not about keeping promises unbroken, but about keeping love alive. Sometimes that requires repair, sometimes concealment, sometimes even transgression. To be faithful is not to remain fixed; it is to remain oriented — to return, again and again, toward what one values most, even if by the most indirect routes.

Emmanuel Levinas once wrote that ethics begins not with rules but with *responsibility before the face of the other*. This responsibility is asymmetrical — we owe it even when we cannot fulfill it, and perhaps especially when we fail. Ethical infidelity belongs to that tragic category. It does not erase responsibility but heightens it: it is the recognition that love's demands exceed human capacity, and yet must still be honored.

To reframe the question, then, is to see that the adulterer's dilemma is not a perversion of ethics but its crucible. In the moment of transgression, one confronts what moral life truly is: not the perfect alignment of desire and duty, but the endless attempt to reconcile them. In that struggle, fidelity reveals itself as something larger than sexual exclusivity — as an existential practice of care that persists even when the rules are broken.

If (as Paul Tillich defined it), sin is separation from God, from others, and from oneself, then ethical infidelity can be seen not as the refusal of connection but as a distorted attempt to repair it. When a marriage has hardened into duty, when tenderness has been dulled by routine, an affair can sometimes become an errant gesture of longing — not for another person, but for the lost feeling of aliveness itself. This does not make it right, but it makes it human.

The question, then, is not whether betrayal can be justified, but whether it can be made *faithful* — whether an act of rupture can still point, however imperfectly, toward the same horizon of care. To betray faithfully is to break one law in order to preserve another, to violate a rule for the sake of a deeper responsibility. It is, in short, to love imperfectly but sincerely.

And so our task is not to moralize or absolve, but to think. To ask: what kind of moral framework can accommodate human weakness without trivializing it? How might we imagine fidelity not as the absence of betrayal, but as the art of returning after it?

Toward an Ethics of Return

Every philosophy begins as an act of inheritance and rebellion. The argument of *Ethical Infidelity* has moved through familiar terrain — Mill's liberal humanism, Nietzsche's vitalism, Freud's account of repression, Kierkegaard's lonely faith, and even the Catholic understanding of confession and grace. Yet what emerges from these crossings is not a synthesis in the usual sense. It is a new moral orientation, one that we might call *The Ethics of Return*.

This ethic begins from a simple observation: that human beings are defined less by the capacity to remain pure than by the capacity to begin again. We fail, we stray, we contradict ourselves — and yet we return. The central moral act is not constancy but re-orientation. The good life is not the life without fracture, but the life that knows how to metabolize fracture into depth.

Mill teaches that freedom's legitimacy rests on the avoidance of harm; yet he assumes that harm is primarily external, measurable. The Ethics of Return extends this: it treats inner harm — the slow corrosion of self or intimacy through repression — as equally serious. There are forms of moral suffocation that do not wound others directly, yet diminish the self that loves them. Ethical infidelity responds to that unseen harm not with indulgence, but with calibration — a private act of repair, not revolt.

Nietzsche, in turn, insists that morality must serve life rather than inhibit it. But where Nietzsche's free spirit breaks entirely with convention, the Ethics of Return preserves what he abandoned: responsibility. It seeks not liberation *from* constraint but vitality *within* it. The task is not to abolish vows but to re-enliven them, to let the forbidden teach us why we made the promise in the first place.

Ayn Rand elevates selfishness to moral principle, grounding ethics in the sovereignty of the self. The Ethics of Return borrows her insistence on integrity but strips it of her contempt for vulnerability. It accepts that self-preservation and care for others are not opposites but intertwined. A self that cannot breathe cannot love; but a self that breathes only for itself dies alone.

Even Catholic moral theology, so often cast as the enemy of freedom, contains an intuition that this new ethic reclaims: that sin is not the final word. Confession is not about punishment but re-entry into communion. The Ethics of Return secularizes this ritual — transforming confession from an institutional act into an interior one. What matters is not forgiveness from above, but integration within: the willingness to face one's imperfection without self-hatred.

Together, these fragments point toward a moral vision that is both modern and ancient: a philosophy of fidelity after failure. It neither glorifies transgression nor fetishizes purity. It understands that love, like character, depends on the rhythm of departure and return — on the courage to risk loss, and the humility to come back transformed.

What distinguishes the Ethics of Return from earlier moral systems is its realism. It accepts that the self is not a fortress but a tide. Desire ebbs and flows, faith wavers, attention drifts. The ethical life, then, is not the maintenance of a fixed state but the practice of navigation — of steering back, again and again, toward care. Fidelity is no longer the opposite of betrayal; it is the discipline of returning despite it.

This framework gives infidelity its strange new dignity. The adulterer who returns with clarity has not undone their vow but renewed it under fire. Their transgression becomes part of the vow's biography — a wound that, if tended well, becomes tissue, stronger than before. In this way, ethical infidelity belongs to the same moral family as repentance, artistic creation, and forgiveness: all are acts that turn error into form.

At its core, the Ethics of Return is a philosophy of *moral metabolism*. It does not imagine purity as the goal of life, but digestion — the capacity to transform contradiction into meaning. To live ethically is not to remain intact but to be capable of being remade.

Faithfulness then, is not a state one possesses but a movement one performs, and that every enduring love must pass, again and again, through betrayal in order to know itself.

The Paradox of Fidelity

Fidelity has long been mistaken for stasis. We imagine it as the calm center of love — a promise held perfectly still against time's erosion. But in truth, fidelity is movement. It is not the absence of change but the art of changing without ceasing to belong. The paradox is that to remain faithful, one must sometimes deviate; to preserve a bond, one must let it breathe.

Every enduring love discovers this paradox sooner or later. The honeymoon ideal — that fidelity means unbroken sameness — is not only unrealistic but inhuman. Desire, by nature, is centrifugal. It strains against enclosure. To demand constancy of feeling is to ask the heart to disobey its own metabolism. Yet to surrender entirely to flux would dissolve the very structure that gives love its depth. The task, then, is not to conquer contradiction but to live within it: to let freedom and form hold one another in tension, like melody and rhythm.

The Ethics of Return treats fidelity not as an oath frozen in time, but as a discipline of renewal. Each act of recommitment — after boredom, resentment, or even betrayal — is a re-enactment of the original vow, but now with knowledge added. The first promise is made in innocence; the second, in experience. This is why a marriage that has survived transgression can, paradoxically, be more honest than one that has never been tested. It knows what it costs to stay.

To betray and return is not hypocrisy, then, but the pattern of all moral life. The religious imagination knew this long before secular ethics did. The fall and the redemption, the exile and the homecoming, are not aberrations but archetypes. Even in the most secular terms, every moral subject lives through this rhythm: failure, remorse, reintegration. What distinguishes the ethical from the cynical adulterer is not the act itself but the use to which it is put — whether the fall becomes a descent into nihilism or an ascent into understanding.

We might think of fidelity as having two registers: *ontological* and *ethical*. Ontological fidelity is the deep structure of attachment — the gravitational field that persists beneath every fluctuation. Ethical fidelity is the practice of honoring that field through conscious acts of return. One may wander from the other's bed, yet remain gravitationally bound to their being. To the moral purist, this sounds like evasion; to the realist, it sounds like life.

There is, of course, danger in this elasticity. To invoke the language of "return" is to risk excusing what ought to be condemned. But the opposite danger — the worship of purity — is no less corrosive. When fidelity becomes an idol, it hardens into surveillance. Love becomes a ledger of infractions. The couple begins to live under mutual audit, each measuring the other's virtue rather than their vitality. In such airless intimacy, the moral ideal itself becomes the agent of decay.

The Ethics of Return therefore refuses both extremes: the libertine's denial of obligation and the puritan's denial of desire. It seeks the narrow path between — a fidelity that can accommodate imperfection without collapsing into indifference. Its emblem is not the unblemished statue but the kintsugi bowl: cracked, repaired, and more beautiful for having been broken.

In this light, infidelity is neither the death of love nor its proof, but its test. It exposes whether the bond was built on possession or on attention. The possessive love cannot survive betrayal because it confuses fidelity with ownership. The attentive love can, because it understands fidelity as care — as the ongoing choice to see the other anew, even after the spell of perfection has broken.

The paradox of fidelity, then, is not that it forbids betrayal, but that it presupposes it. To love another human being is to accept that they will, in some sense, fail you — that they are not an object of control but a companion in contingency. What matters is not whether failure occurs, but how one responds to it. The true betrayal is not the act itself but the refusal to return.

In this way, *The Ethics of Return* redefines what it means to be faithful. It asks not for purity of behavior but for constancy of care. To be faithful is to keep coming back — to the other, to the world, to oneself — after every estrangement.

The next section will extend this idea further: that our moral lives are not corrupted by contradiction but animated by it, and that wisdom in love, as in art, arises from the capacity to fail beautifully.

The Ethics of the Tragic

Every serious morality must learn to speak the language of tragedy. For the tragic condition is not an exception to the human story but its form. We are creatures who aspire to purity yet live amid contradiction. We love, and in loving, harm; we promise, and in promising, deceive. The moral imagination that refuses this complexity condemns itself to sentimentality. The task is not to abolish tragedy, but to draw wisdom from it.

The ancients understood this long before modern psychology gave it names. In Sophocles and Euripides, virtue and ruin are not opposites but twins. Oedipus seeks truth and destroys his life by finding it; Antigone pursues justice and brings about her death. Their tragedy lies not in evil but in excess — in the collision of two legitimate goods that cannot coexist. So too in love. Fidelity and freedom are each sacred; yet to serve one fully is to betray the other. Ethical infidelity is the art of living between them without despair.

To speak of *ethical* infidelity may sound oxymoronic, but so is all human virtue when examined closely. Courage is cruelty to fear. Mercy is injustice to law. Even truth, when spoken without care, becomes violence. Our moral life is not the triumph of consistency but the negotiation of opposites. In this light, infidelity is not the negation of love but its negative space — the shadow that gives contour to the light.

Tragedy also teaches us that knowledge is bought at a cost. Every revelation wounds. The one who transgresses, if they are honest, sees more clearly afterward — not because they are purified, but because they are stripped of illusion. They learn what freedom costs, what intimacy demands, what self-deception feels like when it breaks. The adulterer who returns wiser is not redeemed by their act but transformed by its reckoning. This is why, in the tragic vision, guilt and grace are inseparable. One cannot grow without falling, nor love without wounding.

Nietzsche called this capacity to affirm even one's suffering *amor fati* — the love of fate. To live tragically is to accept that the conditions of meaning include the conditions of loss. Ethical infidelity belongs to this affirmation. It is not a rebellion against morality but a deeper submission to its complexity — a recognition that desire and duty, eros and ethics, are not reconciled once and for all but only lived through, one contradiction at a time.

To call infidelity "ethical" is not to make it innocent. It remains an act of harm, but not necessarily of evil. The distinction is crucial. Harm is the shadow of contact; it is inevitable wherever two lives entangle. Evil is indifference to that harm. The ethical adulterer accepts the wound, measures its reach, and seeks to make something of it — tenderness, gratitude, humility. The cynic, by contrast, denies the wound or multiplies it.

In this way, the tragic view restores dignity to moral error. It tells us that the value of an act lies not only in its conformity to rule but in the consciousness it produces. A transgression that deepens awareness may be morally preferable to obedience that dulls it. This is not moral relativism but moral realism: the admission that knowledge, like love, requires risk.

Art has always been the keeper of this tragic wisdom. Literature's most enduring adulterers — Emma Bovary, Anna Karenina, Giovanni, and even Chloe in Rohmer's *Love in the Afternoon* — do not teach us how to live well; they teach us how deeply we can err while still remaining human. Their failures are mirrors, not manuals. What they reveal is that meaning arises not from moral perfection but from the attempt to live with eyes open amid the ruins of our own contradictions.

That is the essence of *The Ethics of Return*: a refusal to turn away from the mess of desire and guilt, to make of them not scandal but understanding. Tragic wisdom does not ask us to celebrate infidelity, but to see in it a clue to who we are — beings who love beyond our strength, and who must learn to carry the weight of that excess with grace.

The Horizon of Care

When all the grand architectures of morality have cracked, what remains is care.

Not duty, not purity, not even love in its romantic sense — but care as the smallest, hardest act of attention we can still give to another being.

The *Ethics of Return* reaches its horizon here. Every earlier idea — renewal through failure, the paradox of fidelity, the dignity of secrecy — has pointed toward this one truth: that the worth of a life is measured by the tenderness with which it tends to what it has damaged. Ethical infidelity, stripped of provocation, is simply the effort to keep caring even after one has failed to do so perfectly.

Care is what rescues desire from consumption. It is what turns pleasure into relation. The adulterer who returns thoughtfully does not justify his act; he redeems its meaning by converting self-indulgence into renewed responsibility. His attention, newly sharpened by guilt and gratitude, becomes a form of repair. He learns that the truest apology is not confession but gentleness — a tone of voice, a small patience, a refusal to wound again.

To live by care is to accept finitude. It is to know that no one can be everything for anyone, that every bond will fray, that fidelity itself will sometimes fail. Yet care persists where belief falters. It endures without illusion, as an act of quiet maintenance in a world of entropy. One might say that care is the secular grace that succeeds faith: not forgiveness from above, but the steady work of attention below.

This is why ethical infidelity, for all its risk, can belong to the moral life. It is an acknowledgment that eros and ethics share a single ground — the wish to feel alive in relation to another. When that aliveness grows dim, we seek it elsewhere; when we return, chastened, we find that what we sought was never merely pleasure but presence. The affair ends, but the longing to care remains.

In this sense, the horizon of care is not beyond betrayal but through it. To have failed and still wish the other well; to have wounded and still protect; to have strayed and still come home — these are not contradictions but confirmations of love's depth. They reveal that morality's true center is not law but mercy, not vigilance but compassion.

The *Ethics of Return* thus closes where philosophy and ordinary life meet: in the humble, daily work of keeping faith with imperfection. Fidelity is not the triumph of the will over temptation; it is the persistence of care amid the ruins of certainty.

162

What makes a love endure is not its purity but its ability to survive contamination without losing kindness.

The adulterer who acts in good faith — who cheats, as we have said, ethically — does so not because rules do not matter, but because love does. He recognizes that to preserve the spirit of the bond, he may sometimes violate its letter; that his duty is not to the image of innocence, but to the reality of compassion. His fidelity is no longer a fortress, but an act of tending — fragile, provisional, alive.

When the moral languages of purity and confession have run out, care is what remains: the final form of fidelity, and the first.

Epilogue:
The Grace of Failure

I. The Grace of Failure

Every morality must end where life begins again — not in perfection, but in failure.

Failure is the seam that runs through all that is human. We learn by breaking, we grow by misjudging, we love by erring. Yet we spend so much of our lives pretending otherwise — as if purity were possible, as if goodness required never falling short. The deeper truth is more merciful: that what redeems us is not innocence, but our capacity to make something beautiful out of what has been broken.

The argument of this book has never been that infidelity is good. It is that goodness itself is incomplete without an understanding of infidelity — of desire's restlessness, of conscience's fragility, of the soul's appetite for contradiction. To live ethically, under the conditions of being human, is not to obey without exception, but to navigate between fidelity and failure with attention, courage, and grace.

Grace here is not divine but earthly. It is not a pardon from above but a movement within: the capacity to fall without disintegrating, to return without self-contempt. Grace is the quiet intelligence that allows a person to look at what they have done —

the wound, the secret, the compromise — and still choose tenderness. It is the ability to make care survive disillusionment.

To live with grace is to refuse the cruelty of moral purism. The fantasy of purity isolates; it imagines a world where love is clean, desire unbroken, conscience untroubled. But that world would be uninhabitable. The human heart is not a closed system but a weather pattern — it shifts, storms, clears, begins again. Fidelity, in its deepest sense, belongs to this rhythm. It is not the refusal of movement but the promise to return after every change.

The *Ethics of Return*, as this book has called it, is therefore not an ethic for adulterers alone. It is a way of understanding the moral life itself: as a series of departures and homecomings, betrayals and renewals, each deepening rather than diminishing our capacity for care. To fail ethically — to err in good faith — is still to belong to the moral world.

II. The Modern Condition

We live in an age that fears contradiction but cannot escape it.

Our institutions promise transparency, our relationships demand authenticity, our technologies reward self-exposure — and yet our inner lives remain opaque. Never before has honesty been so fetishized, or secrecy so shamed. We confess not to God or to a lover, but to the algorithm. In such a culture, the idea of *ethical infidelity* sounds like heresy because it insists on mystery — on the right to hold something back, not as deceit but as dignity.

Modernity mistakes information for intimacy. We imagine that love will be saved by disclosure, that every secret is a toxin. But love, like art, needs shadows. The Ethics of Return is not nostalgic for repression, but realistic about opacity. It proposes that secrecy, when guided by care, can protect rather than poison;

that privacy is the last sanctuary of sincerity in a world that has turned everything else into data.

This may explain why infidelity — real or imagined — has become one of our last moral taboos. It concentrates all the anxieties of the age: about truth, control, autonomy, and vulnerability. But taboo also signals fascination. Our stories keep returning to the adulterer not because we celebrate betrayal, but because we recognize ourselves in it. We too live in double lives: the person we show and the one who dreams; the life we have and the one we fear losing.

In this sense, *Ethical Infidelity* is less a manual for transgression than a mirror held up to the modern soul. It argues that fidelity is not the opposite of desire, but its highest form — and that the moral life, in a time of transparency, will depend on rediscovering the nobility of discretion.

III. An Author's Note on Ethical Infidelity

This book began with a provocation and ends with a confession: the provocation was intellectual, but the confession is human. The provocation was to ask whether cheating could ever be ethical; the confession is that no philosophy, however elegant, can resolve the rawness of the heart.

What philosophy can do, though, is widen the frame of compassion. It can remind us that people do not cheat simply because they are cruel or weak, but because they are searching — for affirmation, for aliveness, for some fragment of themselves lost to routine. Some searches destroy; others restore. The difference is intention and care.

If this book has argued for anything, it is that our moral vocabulary must grow up. We need a language that can speak of failure without contempt, of secrecy without shame, of desire without panic. The *Ethics of Return* is one attempt at such a language: a small philosophy of human tenderness amid contradiction.

It is not a defense of betrayal but of complexity. It is not an excuse for deceit but a plea for mercy — mercy for those who fall, for those who forgive, and for those who keep trying to love in a world that makes love nearly impossible.

Perhaps, in the end, that is all ethics ever is: the courage to keep returning to care, even after everything has fallen apart.

www.ingramcontent.com/pod-product-compliance
Lightning Source LLC
LaVergne TN
LVHW051410080426
835508LV00022B/3017